"J. R. takes something that seems impossible on the surface and makes it simple. Building on one elementary principle, and his practical, actionable steps outlined, he shows you how to transform any area of your life. It doesn't have to be hard or take a long time with his 5 simple steps to mastering a life worth living."

—Niccie Kliegl, RN, CLC

"It is my honor to endorse the book "Turning Pink Elephants into White Tigers". This book is written with absolute clarity about how to take steps to move through a person's biggest trials and hardships to a place where you can achieve anything you can imagine. I've read many books about "positive thinking", but this book takes your hand and guides you through with an easy to understand roadmap. I highly recommend this book for everyone. There is always something in your life that can be improved, and this well written guide book can help you do that."

—Vickie Knob, Author

"If you're struggling with self-doubt and internal or external obstacles that are holding you back from achieving your dreams (even the dream of being a successful blogger), then read, "Turning Pink Elephants into White Tigers." J. R. will show you how to use tools you never knew you already had, but have been there all along, to empower you to move forward to become successful."

—Jonathan Milligan, Blogger, Writer, Speaker

"Being intentional about what you want is the key to your success. Within the pages of "Turning Pink Elephants Into White Tigers," J.R pulls from more than three decades of experience to provide useful lessons, stories and tools that will get you pointed in the right direction, and on a new path to progress, success and growth."

—Joel Kessel, Strategy & Communications Advisor & Coach; Owner of Kessel Communications

TURNING PINK ELEPHANTS INTO WHITE TIGERS

5 Simple StepsTo Master A Life Worth Living From The Inside Out

J. R. MASON

AUTHOR ACADEMY elite

© 2018 by John Mason
All rights reserved

Printed in the United States of America

Published by Author Academy Elite
P.O. Box 43, Powell, OH 43035

www.AuthorAcademyElite.com

All rights reserved. No part of this publication may be reproduced, stored in a retrieval system, or transmitted in any form or by any means-for example, electronic, photocopy, recording-without the prior written permission of the publisher. The only exception is brief quotations in printed reviews.

Paperback ISBN: 978-1-64085-299-0
HardcoverISBN : 978-1-64085-300-3
Ebook: 978-1-64085-301-0

SEL027000 SELF-HELP / Personal Growth / Success
BUS025000 BUSINESS & ECONOMICS / Entrepreneurship

Library of Congress Control Number: 2018942545

For my wife, Elaine. One of God's greatest gifts.

For all of those who have coached and mentored me.

Thank you.

CONTENTS

Foreword xiii
A Life Worth Living xv
Acknowledgments xxi

PART ONE
THE PRINCIPLE

CHAPTER ONE 3
Pink Elephants and White Tigers

Don't Think of Pink Elephants 4
Years of Experience 5
The Power of the Unconscious Mind:
  How the Unconscious Mind Works 7
The Key - White Tigers with Blue Eyes 9
What Happened to My Clients? 10
What are Your Pink Elephants? 11
The Concept of Intention-Aiming the Arrow 12

CHAPTER TWO 15
Case Study: Tarzan

The Gap.. 15
Response Set 18
    Business is booming, or not 19
    Marital bliss, or not 20
Mindset: The Key to Creating the Life Worth Living 21
    Fixed vs. Growth Mindset 23
    Thoughts: The Seed Bed of the Garden of Life 24
    Beliefs: The Root of All Life Programs 27
    Am I Moving or Standing Still? 27
    Death in the Office 28
    Screen Door Dog 29
    Implied Messages 30
Emotions: Thoughts Create Emotions 31
Actions: Doing Creates Results 34
    A Marital Trigger 39
    "Seek First to Understand, Then to Be Understood" 40
Making More Money 40
    Summary: The Steps 42
    The Sky's the Limit 43

CHAPTER THREE 46
Be Not Afraid

Locus of Control 46
Personal Responsibility 48
Victim Versus Victor 50
Victor or Abuser 51
Positive Versus Negative 52
Case Study: Celeste 52

CHAPTER FOUR 54
A Force Multiplier

Case Study: Sheila 55
Iatrogenesis 57
The Atmosphere 58
A Personal Example 60
A Force Multiplier 61
Systems Theory 62
Quantum Faith 63

PART TWO
THE POWER

CHAPTER FIVE 69
Tools of The Trade

Tool One: Mental Rehearsal 70
    How Does It Apply in Your Life? 71
    How I Learned About and Used Mental Rehearsal 72
    How Can It Work for You? 74
    What If I Can't See Images? 75
    Where in My Life Can I Use it? 76
    Case Study: Sierra 76
Tool Two: The Creative Narrative 79
Tool Three: Grounding and Centering 80
Tool Four: Self Hypnosis 83
Tool Five: Energy Psychology 84
Tool Six: The Intention Question 85
    Research About Questions 86
    What's an Intention Question? 86
    Mother-in-law's Fluorescent Light Fixture 87
Tool Seven: Body Proclamation 88

CHAPTER SIX ... 91
Finding Your Zone: Where the Life Worth Living Happens

The Stress/Performance Curve ... 91
The Zone ... 93
The Wheel of Life ... 95

CHAPTER SEVEN ... 97
Bulldoze the Barricades: Making Easy Work of Obstacles

What Obstacle? ... 97
Use Occam's Razor ... 98
Four Keys to Your Breakthrough ... 104
Alternative Strategies ... 105
Boundaries ... 108

CHAPTER EIGHT ... 111
The Truth About Power: A Little Bit Goes a Long Way

The Problem of Power ... 111
The Power of Follow Through ... 113
Types of Power ... 116
The Spirit Effect ... 130

PART THREE
THE PROCESS

CHAPTER NINE ... 155
Romancing the Pain: Making pain your servant

Your Relationship to Pain ... 155
The Aspects of Pain ... 158
Romancing the Pain ... 160

Secondary Gain 161
Illness Identity Disorder 162

CHAPTER TEN 164
The Purpose of Purpose: Whose Purpose Is It Anyway?

Your Purpose 164
Whose Why Is It, Anyway? 166
Your Purpose is Your Mission 167
Your Identity, A Clue to Your Purpose 168

CHAPTER ELEVEN 174
Time to Transformation: Where Life Begins

Transforming You 174
Transforming Relationships 176
Transforming Business 177

Appendix A: Discussion Points 179
Appendix B: Specific Examples 183
Appendix C: How to Do Body Proclamation, Step-By-Step 188
Endnotes 191
About The Author 199

FOREWORD

I left my day job to pursue my dream job—Igniting Souls. Through writing, speaking, and coaching, I help individuals and organizations clarify who they are, why they're here, and where they should invest their time and energy.

I struggled finding my own distinct voice and passion. As a young man, I suffered from severe stuttering, depression, and self-injury. Today a transformed man, I invest my time helping others become Souls on Fire.

Many who read this book would love to leave their day job and pursue their dream job. Many also struggle with finding their own distinct voice and passion. Perhaps they also struggle with depression, anxiety, and lack of clarity about how to make changes.

It's time to meet your guide J. R. Mason. He's a Soul on Fire. After gaining clarity he was able to draw from over three decades of experience to write a simple, step-by-step process for how to create a new life from the inside out.

In this book he weaves a masterful story forged from personal and professional experience. He's had to apply everything he teaches to get him to where he is today. He also left his day job for his dream job and he is intentional about helping others create a life worth living from the inside out.

Get ready to have J.R. guide you to become a Soul on Fire. You'll soon discover as I did that it all starts from the inside out. Brace yourself for an adventure of a lifetime.

Kary Oberbrunner, author of *Your Secret Name, The Deeper Path, and Day Job to Dream Job.*

A LIFE WORTH LIVING

"The unexamined life is not worth living."

        Socrates, Classical Greek philosopher

"Believe that life is worth living and your belief will help create the fact."

        William James, American philosopher and psychologist

At first glance, these two quotes seem to contradict one another, but in reality, both are accurate. What makes a life worth living for one person when another in similar circumstances is miserable? Where does a person start to create a life worth living?

When I was 17 years old and going through a stressful time, I experienced a period of profound depression. Over time, it seemed to become worse, and eventually,

I began having suicidal thoughts, something I'd never experienced before that point. It had never been like me to be depressed, let alone suicidal.

I recall sitting down at the desk in my bedroom where I usually did my homework with the goal of figuring out what was going on. In my mind, the whole world seemed dark and meaningless. My future looked hopeless and like a black cloud.

There was a desk calendar mounted on my wall with nothing written on it. I used it mainly to track the date. As I stared at the calendar, it came to me; I had nothing fun going on in my life or anything positive to anticipate. The way I was living was stressful, bleak, and miserable.

During the mid 1970's, counseling was rare, expensive, and unreliable, so it wasn't much of an option. Instead, I said a little prayer and decided to come up with my own solution. Within a few seconds, I had an idea.

My idea was to create a list of some enjoyable activities to look forward to doing every day for a week, every week for a month, and every month for a year. At the end of each week, I'd fill in every day of the following week with some positive activity. The process repeated throughout the months in that manner.

I could choose to go for a hike, take in a movie, hang out with friends, go to the river and fish, or anything else. My plan didn't require the days or activities to look any certain way; I could even engage in the same activity for each day of the week.

That's what I did consistently for the next two years. Within three or four weeks, I had no trace of depression remaining. In reality, my state began to shift immediately between having the idea and entering the first activity on the calendar. In a relatively short period,

I went from having a life almost not worth living to have a life well worth living.

When I think back on that time in my life I wonder how I knew what to do and how I was able to create such a tremendously positive result in such a short time. Was it just a coincidence? Did I so happen to have good genes?

No, it wasn't an accident, a coincidence, or good genes. It was the result of subtle, positive influence in my life beginning at a very young age. That influence had been bumping my rudder just outside of my conscious awareness since I was born. I believe that the same force is nudging everyone's rudder every day. For some reason, I resonated with it and benefitted by responding in a proactive way.

No one who knew me at that time would have labeled me an optimist. I was a melancholy person with a decided bent toward the pessimistic.

My earliest definite influence was The Bible. Going to church, listening to my father speak about The Bible, and learning to read for myself sowed many of the seeds for the concepts I was to apply later.

A copy of Norman Vincent Peal's book *The Power of Positive Thinking*[1] showed up in our home and I read that. I also had a handful of influential grade school and high school teachers who thought and taught proactively, and who played supportive roles in my development. Accordingly, when the time came, the seeds were there. After applying the concept in such a primitive way and gaining a significant result, I was impressed.

About the same time, I learned the power of mental rehearsal from a high school teacher and grounding and centering by my karate instructor. I'll tell you more about those powerful tools later in this book.

By the age of nineteen, I'd learned how to efficiently shift my psychological, emotional, and physical state within a few seconds to a few minutes. The same seeds were then harnessed to take me on a journey to college and eventually earn a graduate degree. Along the way, applying similar principles, I met and married my fantastic bride, Elaine.

There have been hundreds, if not thousands, of similar decision points along the way that have had enormously positive results in my life. If I'd mindlessly followed a life script without pro-active decisions along the way, it's entirely possible I wouldn't have been around much longer.

As I entered my twenties, I learned more and more about the power of intention through the teachings of writers such as Napoleon Hill[2] and Robert Schuller[3]. The light bulb was getting brighter and brighter. No longer was it just a subconscious influence; I was noticing a trend that was crystallizing into principle.

In my thirties, I became a counselor and began working with clients based on what I'd learned in school. It didn't work very well, so, I began to apply what I'd used in my teens and twenties. The results were impressive. The traditional school system never taught any of this kind of thinking.[4]

Eventually, I realized how simple the principle is. It's about your focus being in alignment with life instead of death. Although the principle is quite simple and powerful, it seems to be challenging to teach. So many I've shown seem to miss the idea and continue in misery. A minority of others have been astonished at how quickly their lives changed for the better with a small amount of input.

Leverage is the idea of using a small amount of power to create a significant result and apply that to creating a life worth living. That's the main subject of this book.

I encourage you to give it a chance. Keep it simple. One chapter at a time. In you is the power to create a life worth living from the inside out.

In the movie *City Slickers*, the character Curly, played by Jack Palance, kept trying to tell everyone that the secret to life is "just one thing." Everyone wanted to know what that one thing was, but he never quite got around to telling them, dying before he could so.[5]

I believe that what you'll read in the next chapter is that, "one thing," that Curly wanted you to know.

ACKNOWLEDGMENTS

Speaking of leverage, I would like to acknowledge the people who have played the biggest role in moving me forward in writing this book.

My precious wife Elaine who has encouraged me and helped proof read;
Kary Oberbrunner who has relentlessly coached and educated me;
Jonathan Milligan who doesn't even know he helped coach me through some stuck places with his training; and, at least as important is my editor, Gailyc Sonia Braunstein. I couldn't have done this without her.

PART ONE
THE PRINCIPLE

CHAPTER ONE
PINK ELEPHANTS AND WHITE TIGERS

"If you don't know where you're going, you'll probably wind up someplace else."

> Yogi Berra, American professional baseball catcher, manager and coach

My client, Luanne,[6] had been in four rollover accidents in the four years prior to coming to me for treatment. She was the driver in one, sitting in the passenger seat in another, and traveling in the back seat in the other two. As she sat in my office, Luanne wondered if she was cursed, had a target on her back, or perhaps something worse. Each time she was in an accident she was injured a little more seriously than the time before, but she had always recovered. She was afraid to drive anymore.

Luanne reported that since the last rollover, she drove with a tight grip on the steering wheel, telling herself, "Don't drive off the road! Don't drive off the road! Don't drive off the road!" She had a strong sense that she was destined for another accident soon.

In the same way, another client, Martha, noticed a pattern in that every place in which she had lived over the past ten to twelve years had burned down at intervals of about one place every one to three years. When she came to me for help, she was anticipating that it would happen again that year.

Luanne and Martha were stymied. They had each realized that they were the common denominator in the negative events that kept happening to them. They both desperately wanted to know what was going on and what could they do about it.

The answer they were seeking was both simple and profound.

Don't Think of Pink Elephants

"Don't think of pink elephants!"

What happened when you read that sentence? If you're like the majority of people, you immediately began thinking about pink elephants. Congratulations, you're normal!

Now what? You've probably heard the saying that it's all fun and games until someone gets poked in the eye. We all know that getting poked in the eye is no fun at all. It's the same with pink elephants. It's all fun and games until you can't get the pink elephant out of your head.

Have you ever gotten a song stuck in your head? What about a disturbing picture? It's the same thing. Over the years, I've been asked the same question by hundreds of people: what if I don't want to think about pink elephants anymore?

Left to their own devices, most people will admit defeat pretty easily. Even the most determined people will shrug their shoulders and allow that darn pink elephant to stymie them. The answer is deceivingly simple, however, and how you answer can determine the quality of your life from now forward. It's that big of an issue and it's probably the reason you have the experiences that you have right now in life.

What can you do if you don't want to think of pink elephants?

You can admit defeat and accept that you will always think about pink elephants. You can tell yourself NOT to think about pink elephants from now on. You can tell yourself to think about something else. Or, you can change your mindset and change your life.

Years of Experience

I had been a counselor for over three decades, and it took me counseling hundreds of clients, perhaps more, to discover and narrow down the principle of Pink Elephants and White Tigers. My area of specialty was trauma, but I worked with individuals experiencing a wide range of problems. Many came in plagued with anxiety, depression, obsessive thoughts and relationship problems. Cognitive Behavioral Therapy (CBT), a form of talk therapy, helped about twenty percent of them.

Naturally, I wanted to find other techniques to help the other eighty percent. I studied guided imagery, hypnosis, Eye Movement Desensitization and Reprocessing (EMDR), energy psychology, biofeedback and other modalities. EMDR is an enormously useful technique, and the most researched psychotherapeutic technique in history.

After a period of pursuing different "alternative" therapies with my clients for whom CBT did not work, a pattern emerged. About eighty percent of the clients seemed to get better, regardless of the approach that I used. However, there was another twenty percent who didn't seem to progress, regardless of anything therapy tried.

It seemed that of the twenty percent who did not improve, most arrived in my office with a chip on their shoulder, literally "daring" me to help them. It became evident over time to me that getting better was not what they really wanted. Their reason for visiting a professional was to "prove" that even counseling couldn't help them. In their minds, nothing could help.

I took some time to do an inventory of what was working with various clients, and what might be missing. The problem seemed simple: the principle of intention. Those clients who benefited from the work either had the predetermined desire to improve or were easily influenced by my expectation of a positive result (a process called, "iatrogenesis."). The word "iatrogenesis" is derived from Greek and means "brought forth by the healer." In this context, iatrogenesis refers to the manner in which a doctor's expectation of a patient's outcome can affect that patient's health for either good or bad.

Those clients who were intentional about creating results also had a measure of personal responsibility. One can't exist without the other. Properly engaged, personal responsibility is powerful. It's an essential ingredient when being intentional. Positive intentionality can help to overcome anxiety, depression, and self-defeating beliefs and thoughts. In fact, positive intentionality can improve pretty much any area of a person's life.

Since then, the heart and soul of all that I do and teach is positive intention. It's the essence of a positive, proactive and productive life. I call it "Intention Coaching."

In my coaching practice, I make it clear to all of my clients that they are responsible for the results they create in their life. When they change their focus, they improve their lives. The mechanism, such as imagery, hypnosis, EMDR or energy psychology is just icing on the cake and may help massage things along, but positive intention is what will change their lives.

My passion is to pass on **this simple concept, principle, and skill to you so that you may have the wonderful life you want and deserve by being the best you that you can be.**

The Power of the Unconscious Mind: How the Unconscious Mind Works.

Understanding how the human mind is designed is the key to finding the solution. Yes, I said designed, not how the mind has evolved.

In the 1990s, I studied hypnosis. A big part of being a hypnotherapist is learning the "language" of the unconscious mind. Although some hypnotherapists disagree, the human unconscious mind relates best to concepts rather than grammar. So, in our case of a pink elephant stuck in our mind, the grammar of a statement is the instruction to not think of pink elephants. Whether hypnotized or not, your unconscious mind immediately seizes on the verb "think" and the subject, "pink elephants."

Nerve impulses travel at about 300 feet per second in your body, which is essentially immediate. Your unconscious mind seems to bypass the "do not" part of the request. In fact, I believe that your unconscious mind also hears the word "do" and considers the word "not" as undefined, meaning that it might as well not exist.

Accordingly, if I tell you not to think about pink elephants, your mind translates it immediately into an instruction specifically to think about pink elephants. Your mind focuses on the concept of a pink elephant and in effect gives you precisely what you don't want, namely a giant pink elephant.

Additionally, your unconscious mind relates to intensity, which means that the more you don't want to think of pink elephants, the bigger the herd and the brighter the pink! The more you don't want to replay that song, or disturbing image, the louder or more detailed it becomes.

Yet a third aspect that is important about your unconscious mind is that it's also attracted to the specific, which makes sense because it relates to concepts. The more specific a concept is, the more attractive it is to your unconscious mind.

There are other dynamics of how the unconscious mind works, but the three mentioned above are the ones that can most effectively and easily help you change your life. The best way to manage those pink elephants efficiently is to work WITH your unconscious mind's design. You can learn how to harness the dynamics of the unconscious mind for your success. This is powerful to understand and embrace for living the life we want.

The majority of humanity works against itself every moment of their lives. It may seem overly bold, but it's my firm belief that if anyone learns what you're learning in this book and applies it correctly, they will never again need to go to a counselor or psychotherapist. The principles described in this book can help the majority of people overcome anxiety, depression, hopelessness, failure, poverty, conflicted relationships and many other problems.

There's an underlying principle you can follow that will allow you to harness the design of your unconscious mind. It's a straightforward principle that can change your entire life. The majority of humans apply the exact opposite of this principle.

The Key - White Tigers with Blue Eyes

> "We cannot solve our problems with the same thinking we used when we created them."
>
> Albert Einstein, Theoretical physicist who developed the theory of relativity

The **key principle or policy is to focus on what you're for, rather than on what you're against.**

Can something so powerful be that simple? Yes. When I throw that principle out for a person to grasp, the majority of people look at me like I'm crazy. They believe they are already doing that, when they truly aren't. People would not have the problems they do if they already practiced a positive focus, and I would not need to write this book. Be clear about what you'd like to have in place of the pink elephants. An excellent question to ask yourself is what you would rather think about.

For me, the answer is pretty straightforward. I like to think about white tigers with blue eyes. White tigers with blue eyes are very specific. They're attractive. They're engaging. I like to think about them. When I repeat the phrase "think about white tigers with blue eyes," several times, my pink elephants vanish in under three minutes. I do not "get rid of" my pink elephants. Instead, I transform them into what I would rather have in my mind.

Many clients have come into my office and told me they want to "get rid" of their anxiety, depression, obsessional thoughts, relationship problems, financial problems. This list could go on forever. However, getting rid of those things create a vacuum in your mind, and the unconscious mind abhors a vacuum. A negative thought or emotion is at least something to think about, which, for your unconscious mind, is much better than thinking about nothing.

What if you decided you wanted to get rid of your bedroom furniture because it's old, it has some bad memories associated with it, or it's just not working for you anymore? You call The Salvation Army, and they come and pick up your old furniture. Now, you've got an empty bedroom. Imagine walking into the empty bedroom at bedtime. Where would you sleep?

For some of us (mostly guys), that's not a problem. We would either sleep on the sofa in the living room or get a sleeping bag. Of course, you wouldn't really handle getting rid of bedroom furniture that way, but, it winds up being the type of thing many of us do in our minds, leaving a gaping hole for negativity to inhabit.

What Happened to My Clients?

I taught all of this to my clients, Luanne and Martha. They grasped the concept quite quickly but weren't sure what to do about it.

Let's start with Luanne. When Luanne got behind the wheel of a car after her last accident, she would grasp the steering wheel tightly and repeat in her mind, "Don't drive off the road!" What did she not want to happen? She was against driving off the road.

What would she prefer to have happen? She wanted to be safe. I reminded her that she was safe and that she had safely survived each rollover. She thought for a moment and then said, "Well, I want to drive straight." The unconscious mind can also be very literal, so I asked Luanne what she was going to do about curves.

I asked her instead simply to consider the opposite of driving off the road which is to stay on the road. I requested that she create an intention statement of "Stay on the road, stay in the lane," and to repeat it over and over as she drove. I assured her that if she did that faithfully, she would never drive off the road again.

Martha had to rework a belief that she did not deserve to have a beautiful place to live or to have nice things. We created an intention statement of her home being safe and intact at all times and added some positive imagery.

I worked with Martha over ten years ago, and there has been no further incendiary incidents. A small change in one area created a massive change in another area.

What are Your Pink Elephants?

Most of us don't have intense pink elephants like Luanne and Martha, but in their essential form, most of us have the same problem they each had.

As you read on, make a list of the pink elephants in your life. For some, it may be intrusive thoughts that cause anxiety. For others, it may be a pattern of relationship problems, financial problems, emotional problems, health problems, or any other issue that takes over the mind. A pink elephant is anything you've been focusing on trying to get rid of. It's the proverbial elephant in the room, (pun intended) taking up space in your head.

A positive focus means that you are focused on what you want. A negative focus is being focused on what you don't want. A neutral focus means that you have no particular focus.

Having a positive focus is the only way to achieve the goals you have for yourself and to overcome resistance efficiently. Having a negative or a neutral focus is a huge problem. A negative focus can quickly drive you someplace you don't want to be, while a neutral focus leaves you at the mercy of everyone else's more coherent intention.

The Concept of Intention-Aiming the Arrow

"Our intention creates our reality."

Wayne Dyer, American philosopher, self-help author and motivational speaker

The entire process of focusing on what you are in favor of is all about intention. Intention is a word many gurus have used for decades. It's a small word with enormous meaning and power.

The true concept of intention is something more powerful than the manner in which the word is thrown about in our daily lives.

The Latin word for intention is "intentio." It means to "aim at or stretch toward." An example would be an archer aiming their arrow at the bull's eye of a target several yards away. The archer places the arrow carefully onto the bowstring, then lifts the bow and aims the tip toward the bull's eye. The archer's eyes are aimed precisely at the bull's eye, their body facing the exact spot they want their arrow to land.

In reality, a trained archer is also aiming their mind and their soul at the bull's eye, and when all aspects of the archer's mind and body synchronize, that arrow will undoubtedly hit the bull's eye.

There is a philosophy known as teleology. The word "teleology" is derived from two Greek words meaning "goal-directed." It is a philosophy that seeks to explain the reason for something by understanding its purpose or goal in the universe as directed by a conscious, "intentional" being. Of course, that conscious, intentional being is God.

The human mind is also teleological which means that it's goal-directed. Human beings tend to drift in the direction that they're thinking. For example, if you watch enough Taco Bell commercials, you'll soon start thinking about how nice it would be to have a taco. On a conscious level, you might not even realize you just watched a dozen Taco Bell commercials, but suddenly a thought pops into your head that you need a taco right now and you wonder where the thought came from.

The Pennsylvania State University psychology department determined that the average person speaks at about 125 to 169 words per minute, and that the average person thinks at a speed about four times faster than that, which means we think at a speed of about 500 to 676 words per minute.

The dialogue in our subconscious mind is estimated to operate at a rate of about 1,500 words per minute, so the thoughts that are directing our goals and behavior are always there. Whether they are positive, negative or neutral, they are still there.

A good example of this dialogue is what happens when you're driving down the road. Your vehicle will tend to go where your eyes are looking. That's teleology! Some researchers have labeled this "The Moth Effect," and have also called it, "Fascination Phenomenon."[7]

You know the idea; how moths tend to be drawn into a flame to their ultimate doom. The same thing can happen to drivers when a highway patrolman has pulled someone over and their emergency lights are flashing. Some believe that drivers can be drawn into the lights of the patrol car.

It's a researched fact that police cars are involved in more accidents than regular passenger vehicles. However, it's not clear from the research about why this happens.

It's the same when piloting a small aircraft. Flight instructors call it "dead reckoning," or "flying by the seat of your pants," which simply means that the plane will tend to drift in the direction the pilot's eyes are looking.[8]

Being intentional means aiming your eyes, mind, and self at something. The compelling part is that you can choose what that something is. The aim of your mind affects the direction of your life. It is the reason you wind up where you do. In the same way that your aim affects the direction you travel, the goal you set in your mind also plays a crucial role in influencing your state of being. Your state of being can be positive, negative or neutral, and learning how to shift yours as efficiently and quickly as possible is crucial to having a better life.

CHAPTER TWO
CASE STUDY: TARZAN

"You cannot change the wind, but you can adjust your sails."

Unknown

The Gap

There's a gap between where you are and where you'd like to be. To get where you want, the gap needs to be closed. Where you want to be isn't coming to you, so you need to be the one who moves.

Maybe there are two gaps. One is between you and your goal, and the other is between the outer you and inner you. Both gaps must be closed for a successful outcome. When the inner gap closes the outer one will take care of itself.

What would it take for you to have a better life?

There are two options for having that life. Option one is for you to have the ideal circumstances you may have assumed would be involved in having the life you love. An example is how most people think that if they had millions of dollars, a particular car, house, spouse, or a bunch of other stars aligned, they'd have the life they desire.

I heard an interesting statistic a few years ago that over eighty percent of people who win the lottery are broke within 12 months. Further, they're in debt by an additional ten percent of their original winnings. It doesn't seem to matter how much they won.

Their mindset isn't one that's able to comprehend what it is to have and manage wealth. When it's all over many are divorced, have no friends, and may even be addicted to drugs or alcohol. Part of their mind makes sure they get rid of anything that doesn't line up with their pre-lottery identity.

The second is to be transformed from the inside out instead of trying to make circumstances behave. To live this way means to shift how you think, what you believe, and how you feel about yourself, others, God, and the world in which you live.

> "Circumstances are not the problem. Your perception of your circumstances is the problem."
>
> Graham Cooke, Writer and popular conference speaker on the prophetic, spiritual warfare and intimacy with God, leadership, and the next level spirituality

There's a gap in most people's lives between where they are and where they want to be. Most people seem to believe that if they can have the circumstances they want, then they'll love the life they have. However, even if circumstances can be arranged many people continue to be unhappy. Changing the outside isn't the secret to happiness. Successful transformation of your life all begins from the innermost you. It starts with your state. Your mental, emotional, spiritual, and physical states are the condition you're in at any particular time.

Your state can be pro-active, reactive, or neutral. The results created in your life flow forth from within for the good, the bad, or the indifferent. Change your state, beginning with the innermost you, and you change everything.

While you're reading this chapter, keep in mind three common problem areas for most people. Those areas are the personal, business, and relational arenas. In the personal zone, a good example is how you respond to drivers who cut you off in traffic. If that doesn't apply to you, think about how you respond to a specific situation elsewhere in your life that causes problems for you.

As far as business is concerned, think about any struggles that you may have experienced with making enough money, growing your business, and even just having a job you like. In the relational arena, think about marital triggers that lead to arguments, fights, and even divorce.

If none of these seem to apply to you, then ask yourself what area does need to change for you to begin to have the more satisfying life you desire. To change your life, you must begin with changing your response set to any areas of life that aren't working.

Let's bring this back to our case study subject, Tarzan.

I'm given to understand that Tarzan is in pretty decent physical condition (after all, it's hard to believe that the movies and books would lie about such a thing!).

Apparently, Tarzan does a good bit of swinging from one part of the jungle to another. He's pretty good at it. It probably took a lot of practice to get good at it. I mean, it would seem that he may have missed a vine here and there and fallen with an unceremonious thud on the jungle floor now and then (what some who trade in the stock market would call a "dead cat bounce"), perhaps as he was moving from one vine to another with what appeared to be seamless efficiency he was distracted by a pink elephant. Those things happen. We've all been there.

How did he overcome that? I guess that an interview with Tarzan would reveal that he's learned to manage his state pretty well. He probably has a very focused mental, emotional, and physical state. We never seem to hear much about his spiritual state. His relationships with jungle animals and a few natives are known to be pretty healthy.

He didn't get to such an empowered state by accident. He wasn't just born that way. It took a lot of practice. In Tarzan's case, managing his state is key to survival. His survival as well as Jane's, Cheetah's, and others.

Response Set

A response set is any unique, pre-programmed way in which you respond to various situations and people. Are you patient or impatient? Are you impulsive or controlling? Are you anxious or confident? For most of us, the pre-programming occurred early in life. More is caught than taught and most of us wound up catching some pretty serious programming.

As an example of a personal response set, imagine driving along a moderately busy road and just minding your own business. You might be in a mild state of urgency, wanting to be on time to be somewhere. Out of nowhere someone pulls in front of you forcing you to hit your brakes and swerve to avoid a collision.

What's your typical response to that? Some people might become terrified and have to pull over to calm down. Others become extremely angry and stressed out; it ruins their entire day. A few others might chase the offending driver down and try to run them off the road or get into a fight.

Perhaps you've heard the saying "how you do anything is how you do everything." What that means is if you're the type to get angry and let being cut off in traffic ruin your day, you'll tend to respond that way every time it happens. You'll also react the same way to any situation that reminds you of it.

If you're a pink elephant type of person, you'll blame the rude drivers for making you angry and causing you stress. After all, they could have killed someone, or you could fill in the blank with anything else you want. If you're a white tiger type of person, you'll know that practicing the principles and skills in this book can allow you to reprogram your response set to something completely different.

A pink elephant person would find the possibility of reprogramming their response to be incomprehensible and not worth a second thought.

Business is booming, or not

As a second example, think about what you do for a living. Do you love what you do? Some people do. They're blessed! The majority of working adults dislike what they do every day. Some of them make seriously good money, too, but they're stuck because they make too much money to justify quitting. It's known as "golden handcuffs."[9]

If you're a business owner, how's business? Is it booming? Do you love it? Even if you're in a business that you thought you'd love, attracting customers and making money are entirely different subjects than "what" you do.

A pink elephant person will continue in a job that they hate, being miserable, just because of how much money they make. They may also justify staying because of the benefits or for job security. The white tiger person knows they can create a job that's honestly an expression of who they are and what they want. They can work with customers and clients that they love and who love them. They can make as much money as they desire.

The difference between pink elephant and white tiger people is how they choose to program their response set.

Marital bliss, or not

Imagine that you've been married for a while. Now and then your spouse says or does something that "ticks" you off or "hurts" you. You get angry and start speaking to them aggressively. They get mad, and a big argument ensues.

If you're a pink elephant person, you'll blame your spouse for the argument. It will all go downhill and can lead to years of misery and possibly divorce. If you divorce and remarry, it starts all over again with your new spouse. Like thousands of other pink elephant people, you'll *swear* you've done everything in your power to handle the situation, and nothing worked. At first, you conclude that your spouse is a jerk. As time goes by, it seems that everybody but you is a jerk. As a white tiger person, you realize that you can change your response set to your spouse and have it be anything you'd like it to be, regardless of whether or not they ever change.

Is it too soon for me to let you in on a little secret? When you change yourself, your spouse will probably change, too. You just need to go first.

Mindset: The Key to Creating the Life Worth Living

> "All our life transformations come from a renewed mindset."
>
> Graham Cooke

Tarzan's not the only one who would testify to how important to your success it is to be in a focused, empowered state. Any professional or Olympic athlete would say the same thing. They train incessantly to achieve a peak, intentional state to accomplish what most others in the world can barely imagine.

Thousands of such athletes have been interviewed and when asked how they get past distractions and obstacles, almost all say it's the focus of their mindset. When successful people are interviewed, whether they be business people, musicians, artists, etc., they agree it's the mindset that makes the difference.

Mindset refers to the bias of your thoughts, perceptions, interpretations, and beliefs. A mindset can be positive or negative. It can be rational or irrational. It can be effective or ineffective. A mindset can be focused or easily distracted. It can be determined or doubtful.

Your mindset is the *state* of your mind. The state of your mind influences all other aspects of your overall state, beginning with emotions. Emotions are the second most influential aspect of your state.

Remember my client, Luanne, who had trouble with car accidents? She is proof that by changing your focus from what you're against to what you're for, you can literally reprogram yourself – in her case, to drive your car more safely. That simple change of focus virtually eliminated all future rollover accidents that would have happened with the old focus. Following her example, not only can you drive your vehicle more safely, you can respond to other drivers who cut you off with peaceful, patient calmness. Is your mind blown yet?

Changing your focus can shift you into flying an aircraft more accurately and safely, too. It's what I used to get my pilot's license. With properly developed focus you can master virtually anything. It's so simple, yet so powerful. A small change in the direction that your mind is thinking can create a huge change elsewhere in your life. That's serious leverage.

It's like the power of a lever or a pulley. A pole and another rock can move a large boulder using a fraction of the energy that it would take with brute force. A series of pulleys and rope can be used to pull a multi-ton vehicle up a hill with a fraction of the energy that would be needed if it were pulled or pushed directly. A small amount of money can be leveraged into a multi-million-dollar portfolio and significant passive income. If done carefully, you could completely bypass having any money at all come out of your pocket.

Harnessing this power of leverage is key to creating a life you love starting from the inside out. If it doesn't start from the inside out, from the innermost you, it will not happen. Starting from the inside out means beginning with your thoughts.

Fixed vs. Growth Mindset

> "The moment we believe that success is determined by an ingrained level of ability, we will be brittle in the face of adversity."
>
> Josh Waitzkin, American chess player, martial arts competitor, and author

In an important TEDx talk on YouTube called, *The Power of Belief-Mindset and Success*, Mr. Eduardo Briceno[10] outlines the distinction between a fixed mindset and a growth mindset.

He tells the story of Josh Waitzkin, a world-renowned chess master. Mr. Waitzkin learned, "how to learn and succeed and apply that learning to other domains." He was able to go on and master other areas of life besides chess. Mr. Waitzkin realized that the key trap to avoid is believing you are special. If somebody believes that they're better than other people and that they don't have to work hard, they'll never be able to grow. In his talk, Mr. Briceno points out that research shows trying to develop grit or persistence is not nearly as important as the mindset that underlies them.

The good news is that we're not chained to our current capabilities, and that neuroscience research indicates the brain is malleable, which means that we can change our own ability to think and to perform.

A fixed mindset person is worried about how smart they look. If they hit a roadblock on their path to success they interpret that as meaning that they're incapable, so will tend to lose interest in order to protect themselves from being embarrassed. On the other hand, a growth mindset person realizes that effort is what makes them "smart." Their big question is how can they learn. They realize that setbacks are considered to be a normal, healthy part of growth.

Briceno and Waitzkin recommend, based on studies with children, that parents make feedback to be process-related with their kids, meaning they should give feedback based on how hard the child worked to figure out a solution rather than focusing on how innately intelligent they are.

The additional good news is that because the brain is malleable, even older people can change their mindsets. To use a popular colloquialism, even old dogs can learn new tricks.

Thoughts: The Seed Bed of the Garden of Life

> "The ancestor of every action is a thought."
>
> Ralph Waldo Emerson, American essayist, lecturer, philosopher and poet

Starting from your innermost part means that action must begin in your mind and your will. Your will is your intention. Action begins with thinking it and expecting it. The Bible refers to the center of your will as your heart.[11]

Your thoughts refer to your perceptions, interpretations, beliefs, and intentions. A belief is an agreement that you've made with a perception or understanding. The belief can be either true or false, rational or irrational. Beliefs can work in your mind like a computer. They can be conscious or unconscious. They can network together to create a belief system.

Once established, **beliefs play an enormous role in your self-image, self-esteem, and the sense of purpose**

in life. In fact, negative belief systems can be like the root system of Bermuda grass, invading all areas of the lawn that is your life.

"Intention" comes from the Latin word "intentio." It essentially means to "aim at or stretch toward." It's an archery term. An archer "intentios" the bull's eye of a target. The word "intend" is used in this book in its most powerful sense, namely to aim at a goal with the absolute, crystal clear determination of achieving the goal. There is no hesitation, doubt, or wavering. It's already a done deal.

The level of determination is a level of maximum commitment. In a bacon and egg breakfast, the chicken is involved, but the pig is committed. You're all in. The state of your thoughts and intention determine the state of every other area of your life. It's the condition you're in at any given moment.

> "Out of the abundance of the heart, the mouth speaks."
>
> Paraphrase of Luke 6:45

> "A tree is known by its fruits."
>
> Paraphrase of Luke 6:44

It all flows from your innermost being outwardly. The fruits (or results) that you're producing in your life are directly proportional to the quality of your state. Thoughts include your intent, perceptions, interpretations, beliefs, and decisions. Any of those can be either positive, negative, or neutral. Positive thoughts result in positive emotions and positive response sets. In the same way, negative thoughts result in negative emotions and response sets. Neutral thought processes lead to being lead around by a ring in your nose by other people.

Most people fail to have the life they would love because they continually try to intervene too far downstream. They futilely attempt to make circumstances and other people behave to get what they want, only to be disappointed and have it all fall apart.

To make a real difference in your life, you must begin where the stream starts, and the flow starts with your innermost thoughts. Changing the state of your thoughts and your intention transforms the rest of your life. Everything in life begins at the headwaters. The quality of your thoughts and intention determines the quality of results. The 'quality' of your thoughts refers to whether they are positive, negative, or neutral.

A positive intention means being focused on what you're for, what you want, rather than what you're against, or what you don't want. A negative intention means being focused on what you're against, to the exclusion of what you want. Neutral is the same as being out of focus. When you're in a neutral intentional state, you're choosing to have no focus, and you're subject (or servant) to the whims of others who are more focused. Your focus can be clear, partially focused, or unclear. It can be positive, negative, or neutral. It can be powerful or powerless.

The condition of your intention determines the quality of outcome in your state and your life. To have the life you love means to take full responsibility for any of your thoughts, perceptions, interpretations, beliefs, and intentions. Awareness of your thoughts is one of the many forms of power you possess. Learn in the following pages the step-by-step process to transform any thought stream into the direction that you would prefer it to go.

Beliefs: The Root of All Life Programs[12]

A belief is an opinion about something that you've decided is correct, something you've accepted as fact. Whether or not it's true, or whether it's partially true, is irrelevant. If you think the belief is correct then your mind, your emotions, and your body will respond as if it's true.

That's a lot of power. It's a power that can work both for and against you.

Am I Moving or Standing Still?

As I was driving a few weeks ago, I had a bizarre experience. It's happened before, and I'll bet it's happened to you.

I had come to a complete stop with my foot on the brake. My foot started to push harder on the pedal, yet I felt like I was moving. It felt like I was out of control. Although "out of control" isn't a feeling, but a belief, it's common to express it as a feeling.

Then it occurred to me. It wasn't me who was moving. The vehicle next to me was slowly drifting backward. The difference between my experience and the reality of the other car's movement had created an illusion that my vehicle was moving forward, so my body automatically reacted by pressing down harder on the brake pedal. My brain was able to realize that something wasn't right and had to check out what was going on.

The disorientation was temporary due to an illusion, and the illusion was the result of a belief I accepted. My semi-conscious perception of what was happening resulted in a misinterpretation. Somewhere in my brain

I agreed with the perception, and the rest of my mind and body went with along it. My interpretation of that perception was incorrect. Therefore, my attempt to compensate (by pressing on the brake) was meaningless and the result of a false understanding.

This simple example illustrates how quickly beliefs are created, how they affect us every day, and how they can change the course of our entire lives. Beliefs can shut us down or free us up. They can even kill us or heal us. Beliefs can make the difference between poverty and wealth.

Death in the Office

A lot of people still have a hard time believing that so much of their life and emotion stem from their beliefs. There's a little exercise I've used in my office for years to demonstrate how it works. Imagine that you and I are sitting in an office. Assume I've convinced you that the doorknob has a 50,000-volt charge and if you touch it, you'll die. At the same time, I've convinced you the windows and walls are unbreakable. Suddenly, flames shoot out of the air-conditioning vent in the ceiling. I tell you there's no way out and you're going to die. How do you suppose you might feel?

Most people would say scared, panicked, worried, or something similar. How do you think you would feel?

Then I say I was just kidding and flip a switch, activating a fan to suck out the flames and smoke. I explain that the windows and walls are breakable and that the doorknob is perfectly safe.

Now how do you feel? Most people would use words like relieved, angry (that I deceived them) or safe. Finally, I ask them to explain why their emotions changed so dramatically within about 3 minutes. Some people responded by saying that they're no longer in danger, however the reality is they were never in danger. Only one thing changed in those 3 minutes: their BELIEF!

When people believed they were in danger, they felt some form of fear. Even though the threat didn't exist, the belief created the emotion of fear. When people believed they were safe and not in danger, they felt relief.

Isn't that amazing that a very intense emotional state changed from one extreme to another in about 3 minutes. It didn't take years of psychotherapy and working to overcome a trauma that might have happened in childhood. The change merely involved rapid adjustment to agree with a perception.

Your beliefs work together to become what Mr. Bob Proctor[13] calls a paradigm. A paradigm is the logical flow of thought, belief, and action that comes from agreement with your perceptions. The paradigm programs all of your emotional responses and life choices, and it must be shifted for actual change to take place.

Screen Door Dog

A few years ago, I was watching an episode of *America's Funniest Home Videos*.[14] They were showing a clip of a scene at the front door of a person's home. It was the main entry door. The storm door was shut, but the main door was open. The glass panel in the lower half of the storm door was removable.

Outside, sitting by the front door wanting to come into the house, was a cute,

mid-sized dog. A very obedient dog. The owners opened the front door, and the dog came in. They opened the door again, and the dog went back outside and waited. The owners then removed the glass panel from the bottom of the storm door. The dog could easily have walked through the opening and entered the home, but no matter how much they coaxed the dog, it would only come into the house when they opened the storm door. The owners even stepped back and forth through the opening and encouraged the dog to join them. The dog just looked at them and waited until the door was opened before entering or exiting.

The point is that the dog perceived a limitation that wasn't there. The dog believed there was a block even though there wasn't.

Unfortunately, humans can be that way, as well. Even when there is no limitation in our way and all we have to do is walk through the opening, we don't. We wait for some other condition to occur that may or may not happen.

Implied Messages

An implied message is a message that's implied, not directly stated.

What in the world does that have to do with beliefs? A lot. The majority of human beings operate on beliefs about themselves derived from implied messages, namely the belief that somebody else said or implied something seeming to suggest that the other person isn't good enough or that they're a failure.

Communication is 15% verbal and 85% non-verbal. Messages contain both content and process. There's the message, then there's the delivery. A simple message such as "Would you like to sit in that chair?" could be taken more than one way depending on the facial expression, tone of voice, and inflection of the speaker. Said one way it could seem like a very pleasant invitation to sit in a particular chair. Conveyed another way it could sound like an intense disapproval of someone's choice of a particular chair. Any message conveyed by the process rather than the content is called the implied message. Implied messages are subject to any number of interpretations.

There are two aspects to an implied message. The first part is what the speaker is implying; the second part is the message the listener hears. Over ninety-five percent of the time, what the speaker is trying to say is completely different than what the listener interprets. That's a big problem.

If you're a pink elephant person, you'll focus on a negative interpretation and become reactive. You'll tend to assume that you couldn't possibly be wrong. When you operate based on an incorrect, negative interpretation the results will always be negative. The best remedy is to find out what the other person actually means and operate on that. If the situation doesn't involve a person, err on the side of the most positive interpretation.

Emotions: Thoughts Create Emotions

Blossoming from the seedbed of your innermost thoughts is the flowering fruit of your emotions. They must be wonderful, because we all know fruit is wonderful, right? Some people call them feelings. Although to some experts there's a difference between emotions and feelings, for purposes of our discussion, let's just consider them to be the same thing.

Emotions are states such as anxiety, fear, anger, happiness, joy, surprise, sadness, and so on. Other words, such as hunger, unsafe, stressed, and comfortable, aren't emotions, they're opinions, perceptions, or beliefs. In other words, they're thoughts. It's important to distinguish between emotions and thoughts. Being clear about the distinction improves your differentiation, and a highly differentiated person is a significantly more effective and powerful person.

The first step in solving a problem is to accurately identify and define the problem. If you're unclear about whether you're correcting a thought or an emotion, you'll be unsuccessful at finding a solution. All emotions arise from your beliefs, and beliefs are the cause of your feelings. If you change your thinking, you change how you feel. It can change your life.

Not all emotions are "just" emotions. There are primary, secondary, and tertiary emotions. There are also euphemisms. It's believed that there are only about six basic emotions. Depending on who you read or listen to as to which six are considered official. For ease of reference, let's say the official six are fear, anger, sadness, happiness, surprise, and disgust.

Any other feeling words that we use besides those are called euphemisms. A euphemism is just using a mild word or expression to as a substitute for another word considered too harsh or blunt.

A good example is the primary emotion of fear. Common euphemisms are anxiety, dread, horror, stress, and so on. However, psychologically speaking, the distinction made between fear and anxiety is that fear is an alarm response to an identifiable threat, such as an angry, coiled rattlesnake within striking distance that's ready to strike.

Anxiety, in contrast, is the same alarm response a person has who merely hears the word, "snake," even though no snakes are anywhere within miles. There's no present, identifiable threat. Anxiety is more of a conditioned response to a particular trigger word such as "snake." In either case, anxiety is an emotional response to a perceived threat whether real or not.

Emotions play a significant role in the life you've already created for yourself. Many people tend to design their lives around how they feel and expend enormous energy avoiding what they believe will make them feel uncomfortable. Your beliefs create feelings. Your feelings can lead to the creation of a new level of belief. It's a vicious cycle.

For example, if Miss Snake Phobia from the example above has an anxiety response when someone mentions the word snake, she's likely to believe that the very presence of anxiety is proof that there's some form of danger. That proof manifests as a new belief that there's a real danger, even though there are no snakes. Miss Snake Phobia's increased anxiety based on the evidence amplifies her belief and can spiral into a panic attack. When she observes herself responding in that way, she may develop a belief about herself that she's weak or powerless.

In the case of Miss Snake Phobia, the process from belief to feelings might look like this:

Belief: Snakes are dangerous. If one bites me I might die a slow, agonizing, painful death.

=>

Emotion: Fear

=>

Belief response: See? The fear proves it. I wouldn't feel fear if the belief weren't true.

=>

Emotion: Anxiety. Panic.

=>

Belief: I need to panic whenever I hear the word snake, just to make sure I'm on red alert. Just to be on the safe side.

=>

Thus, the downhill spiral begins.

The most important point here is how Miss Snake Phobia's negative perceptions and beliefs can create a spiral of negative, disempowering emotions. The compounding of one false belief on another mixed in with a bunch of negative emotions creates a belief system. A belief system can be complicated to change once it's entrenched, however, it is possible.

Miss Snake Phobia's negative belief system can now affect every aspect of her state -- psychologically, emotionally, physiologically, spiritually, and so on. Her belief system is more or less self-reinforcing. That negative process can affect your choices, how much money you earn, the quality of your marriage, what kind of friends you choose, and even your physical health.

Actions: Doing Creates Results

"After all is said and done, more is often said, than done."

Unknown

After all thoughts, feelings, words, and plans, everything boils down to action. What you do, determines the quality of results, and it's challenging to sustain consistent action if it's not in harmony with who you are. As I've said previously, your state reflects the quality of your thoughts, emotions, and physiology at any given moment, which is why it's vital that you transform from the inside out to create and sustain the life you love. Otherwise, it's like putting a bandage on a broken leg – it's not going to do much good.

A good example is if you've ever tried to overcome a bad habit. The bad habit could be smoking, drinking, cussing, forgetting things, locking your keys in your car, procrastination, or many others. When you attempt to use force to overcome a smoking habit, it doesn't work too well if your underlying beliefs, intentions, and emotions are out of alignment with your goal. Your unconscious mind is a thousand times more powerful than your conscious mind. If your unconscious mind is instructing you to smoke when your conscious mind is telling you to quit, the unconscious mind will win every time. On the other hand, if you've gotten your internal beliefs, intentions, and emotions all in good shape, but take no action, you'll tend to drift back toward where you were in the beginning.

Words plus actions seem to create movement in the quantum field. That's the invisible energy field that permeates the entire universe described by quantum physicists. Such physicists have discovered that subatomic particles respond to being observed by the scientist. Thus, the thoughts and intentions of the observer can affect the behavior of the particles. Much has already been written on this subject by others.[15]

Your thoughts, intentions, and words affect matter. Does this sound familiar? Jesus said that you could tell a mountain to be removed and cast into the sea and the mountain will obey if you have faith as tiny as a mustard seed and do not doubt in your innermost being (your heart). Apparently, Jesus wasn't speaking figuratively, but literally. Quantum physicists are technically confirming what Jesus was teaching long ago.

How others respond will tend to be congruent with the quality of your actions. For example, if you teach a course with the hope of making more money, but the course isn't what they want or need, then they won't respond favorably. On the other hand, if you provide a course, or some other product, that resonates intensely with precisely what others want and need, you can become wealthy. However, just sitting around thinking about it is unlikely to inspire people to send you money.

Here are some practical examples lifted from everyday life.

Being cut off in traffic. Are you the person who gets angry when someone cuts you off in traffic? How can you transform that response set?

Start with what you've learned in Chapter One. After you've evaluated how you tend to respond, the next logical step for transformation is to ask yourself how you would rather respond. It's powerful to write it down on paper instead of just juggling it in your head. Write down exactly how you'd prefer to respond. What actions would be more in your best interest? What feelings would serve you better? What would you choose to believe or interpret about yourself, the other driver, and the situation?

This process isn't always as natural as it would seem. If someone claims to feel angry when cut off in traffic, it can be a struggle to find a replacement for anger. Seeing someone in the throes of such anger, the look on their face seems to imply the message that anger is all there is. What else could there possibly be? Merely realizing there IS another possibility is the first baby step toward a transformed life.

To find out what else there could be, grab your smartphone, iPad, or computer and look up the antonym for anger.

Here's a list I found online at http://www.thesaurus.com/browse/anger:

Antonyms for anger
- calm;
- calmness;
- cheer;
- comfort;
- delight;
- ease;
- glee;
- goodwill;
- happiness;
- joy;
- kindness;
- liking;
- love;
- peace;
- pleasure;
- agreeability;
- contentment;
- enjoyment;
- good nature;
- pleasantness.

It looks like there are a few excellent choices. In fact, there are more than enough choices to ruin a perfectly good blue funk. Anger can feel strong. The idea of replacing it with something else may bring up the concern of feeling powerless or vulnerable. By that,

I mean that some people don't want to give up their anger. They kind of like it. It can be pretty cozy being the victim. Everyone else gets to be wrong, and you get to be right.

Giving up your anger will require a decision to be okay with giving up any perceived benefits of keeping your anger. If you've decided to be a victor instead of a victim and you're ready to move forward, just choose the word on the list that you resonate with the most.

Let's say you've chosen the word calm. Write it out on paper.

"Whenever anyone cuts me off in traffic, I immediately feel calm."

Write it any way you like; just be sure you write it as a positive instead of a negative -- how you want to feel instead of how you don't want to feel.

Next, add something like, "Not only do I feel calm, I immediately and comfortably slow my vehicle down to create a safe distance. I instantly forgive the other driver and release them to travel on down the road. I pray that they'll calm down and be safe as well as everyone else they encounter being safe."

Play around with it until you've got it just the way you'd like. Once you've worded it the way you want, it'll begin to set into motion forces and factors in your unconscious mind that will start to re-program how you respond to being cut off in traffic. Add to the above process the power of mental rehearsal. Create a short video snippet in your mind of being cut off in traffic while feeling completely calm, caring, and confident. In your rehearsal, you imagine yourself merely easing back to give distance while having only the best wishes for the other driver.

To enhance mental rehearsal even more, learn how to ground and center and include that in your mental rehearsal. It's powerful. There's more about grounding and centering discussed in Chapter 5.

A Marital Trigger

What about a negative situation in a marriage? A lot of marital arguments and fights are triggered by the same precipitating event each time. You may not know precisely when it's going to happen, you just realize that it is going to happen. For example, your spouse says something in a particular tone of voice. You feel hurt and begin arguing. They argue back, and the cycle escalates, resulting in a strained relationship. After years of this happening, it's common for couples to throw in the towel and eventually divorce. They blame their spouse. They're certain their next partner won't be like that, but, within two years the cycle has started all over again in their next relationship.

As Walt Kelly said, "We have met the enemy and he is us."[16] Change the cycle by changing yourself, and stop blaming your partner. You can change the entire cycle by changing you from the inside out in the same way that you can reprogram yourself to respond entirely differently to someone who cuts you off in traffic.

Write out a description of how the typical cycle starts and gradually unfolds. Leave out any vindictive remarks. Just write the facts. Next, write down how you'd prefer to feel and respond when your spouse says whatever it is that upsets you. Be specific about how you'd like to feel. Write down a description of you doing a stellar job of accurately listening to your partner and understanding them to their satisfaction.

"Seek First to Understand, Then to Be Understood"[17]

I discovered in all of my training in communication and my experience with over a thousand couples that if one of you, or both of you, are truly understanding the other person to their satisfaction, an argument cannot occur. If you don't believe me, try it. Instead of focusing on forcing them to understand you, choose humility and accurately understand them instead. Let go of any concern about whether or not you agree with them. At this point, agreement is irrelevant. Mentally rehearse feeling calm, centered, and full of love as you imagine them saying that thing that upsets you. Feel it and believe it.

After you've rehearsed it 10 to 12 or more times a day, within a couple of weeks, you'll automatically begin to respond the way you've imagined. The old way of behaving will be disabled and replaced with the new. Keep it up. Don't stop mentally rehearsing. Choose another trigger and repeat the process. In so doing you can turn a bad marriage into a good marriage and a good marriage into a great marriage.

Making More Money

Samantha had been in the people-helping field for most of her life. She was now in her forties. In her whole life, the most she'd ever made was $35,000 a year, regardless of the fact that she had a strong work ethic and was a great person all around. She knew she had some self-limiting beliefs about money but was having a hard time figuring out precisely what they were. What was clear to her was how guilty she felt about having too much money.

We worked together on and off for several months narrowing down and clarifying her limiting beliefs about herself, money, God, and other people. She also developed more clarity about how she'd rather believe about those areas. Samantha read more about the power of intention. Together we clarified more of the truth about herself, money, and her purpose in life. Our work wrapped up around September of that year, and we set up an appointment for February of the following year so she could let me know what happened.

Astonished is the word that best describes Samantha's state when we got together. She'd just had her taxes done, and it turned out that she'd made $50,000 the year she did her work with me! She was almost speechless. She didn't think she'd done anything differently that year than any other. As she discussed her decisions for that year, she realized the choices she'd made were subtly different than usual.

It occurred to her that if she could make $50,000 per year, she could probably make more. I reinforced that belief for her, and we talked about making some adjustments in her thoughts, emotions, intentions, and actions. She decided to target $75,000 for the next year. I never did hear back from her, which tells me that she probably hit a wall regarding how much change she could tolerate for that time in her life. Could Samantha have made $75,000 the next year? Of course! If she took the steps necessary she could make as much as she was able to receive.

I recall reading somewhere that eighty percent of the United States population makes less than $50,000 per year. Some people think it's because greedy people have hoarded all the money, but it's my opinion that nothing could be further from the truth. The fault is not the upper twenty percent of earners; it's the mindset of the eighty percent, which is self-limiting. However, any self-limiting mindset can change when somebody who wants to transform it is willing to do what it takes.

Summary: The Steps

I've just given you three examples, one for each major area of life for most people: personal, relational, and financial. Of course, there could be many more areas to examine, such as health, career, emotional, and spiritual areas. Which area isn't working for you? What obstacles are in your way to having that area work for you?

To transform any area of your life that's not working into one that is working, follow these five steps.

Step One: Notice the pattern. What's happening in the area that's not working for you? Be objective. Keep emotion out of it. Imagine you're a fly on the wall observing. Take notes on what happens first, second, third, and so on. Just look at the *what* for now.

In the traffic example, you're merely driving along. Someone pulls in front of you. You've been startled by it and become angry. Note the series and order of thoughts, emotions, and actions that you've typically taken. There's no judgment, just facts.

If you get hung up on emotions, ask yourself a couple of clarifying questions. The first is what this type of event means to you. The next question to ask yourself is what this type of event means about you. Write out anything that comes up. Those questions are helpful because they can help you tease out irrational beliefs that are driving your emotions and responses set.

Step Two: When it's all described, take a deep breath and ask yourself what it would look like if you could handle this specific situation any way you would like and in such a way as is truly good for you and others. What would that look like?

Write down all ideas that come up. Identify a better replacement, what you'd rather believe, feel, and how you'd prefer to respond. Time is on your side here. Don't rush and keep it as simple as possible.

Step Three: Once you've written it down and put it in final form, read it out loud over and over several times a day. In the traffic example, you could sit in the driver's seat of your car with the engine off, parked in your driveway, and rehearse the scenario playing out exactly the way you've imagined it in your transformed situation.

Check out how it's going for you. If you're having trouble overcoming disturbing emotions or blocking beliefs, learn how to use Emotional Freedom Technique[18] or find someone who uses Psych K.[19]

Step Four: Notice what happens the next time someone cuts you off in traffic. Did it go as you'd rehearsed? If you've been faithfully practicing, then your response will be different. Once you get home, review it in your mind and ask yourself if you need to make any changes to your mental rehearsal and simulator practice.

Step Five: If all went well, celebrate! You've just successfully transformed a part of your life that wasn't working. Afterward, find another area to change.

Keep going until you have a life worth living from the inside out.

The Sky's the Limit

Now you have examples of how to transform your response set to someone pulling in front of you in traffic, to toxic transactions in marriage, and to making more money. These are only three examples; any area of your life can be transformed in a similar way. Think about where in your life you need change from negative to positive, or from bad to good. It's a short jump from there to go from good to great. Would a transformation in those areas get you closer to having a life worth living? Which area needs some TLC first?

The three main areas in which most people need transformation are health, wealth, and relationships. There are all kinds of combinations within those areas that keep the majority of the human race stuck. Each of those combinations represents areas affected by your mindset, your emotions, and your actions. A reworking of your mindset will create an improvement in any area of your life.

Here are a few examples that seem to be very common. Do any apply to you? Are there any that you're experiencing that you could add to the list?

- Lacking self-confidence. For example, self-confidence tied to being perfect or having a certain level of financial success;
- Fear of failure;
- Fear of success;
- Being dependent on unhealthy people;
- Feeling obligated to make others happy;
- Being indecisive;
- Poorly managing time;
- Poorly managing space;
- Lack of follow through;
- Repeating pattern of arguments or fights with others including marital partners and children.;
- Having difficulty breaking out above a certain income level.

If you're not sure which one applies to you or where to start, begin by asking yourself what it is that you'd like to be different in your life. Then, ask yourself what seems to be holding you back from achieving that goal, Whatever the answer is, write it down.

"Never, never, never give up."

> Winston Churchill, British politician, officer and writer; Prime Minister of the United Kingdom, 1940-45 and 1951-55

CHAPTER THREE
BE NOT AFRAID

Locus of Control

"Change your thoughts, and you change your world."

> Norman Vincent Peale, American minister and author

Feeling anxious or fearful is a typical state problem for a lot of people. It was even a problem for a few people mentioned in The Bible. I've read The Bible many times in my life, and each time I've read it, I've noticed something I'd missed in the past.

A few years ago, I was re-reading the Gospels. One morning, a pattern jumped out at me. Sometimes, when an angel would visit a person, the angel would proclaim, "Be not afraid!" I thought to myself that it was a little late for such a warning when the person being visited was already face down on the ground in terror.

Quite a few clients with whom I've worked have struggled with a long history of chronic, severe anxiety. Several of them have stories of years of going to pastors for help and begging God over and over to remove their torment. Too many well-meaning pastors have accused them of not having enough faith. By the time they come to me, they're plagued with anxiety and guilt, and both emotions keep growing.

The implication in the advice given by some pastors is that God has the power to remove their anxiety if they have enough faith. Unfortunately, that hasn't happened, and they're starting to wonder if what they've been believing is true. If they believe The Bible teaches that God will remove their anxiety simply if they have enough faith then apparently that belief is false. As far as I know, The Bible doesn't teach that. Of course, it might also be a problem of not precisely understanding what faith is in the first place.

What the angel said was, "Be not afraid," which suggests that the ability to be unafraid (the "anxiety off" switch) is located somewhere within the human who is on the ground in terror. The location for the ability to change being afraid to being unafraid is called the "locus of control" (the switch is inside of us, not outside of us). If we keep looking for the switch outside of us, we'll spend a long time searching because it's not there.

After applying what could be called *The White Tiger Principle* with these clients, their anxiety diminished steadily until, in most cases, it was completely gone. For some, it took just minutes! When the anxiety is gone, some clients can become confused and frustrated, wondering why the anxiety went away after just a few sessions (or minutes) with me helping them, but nothing happened when they begged God to take it away for years. Others asked why it didn't happen after seeing a whole series of counselors, medical doctors, or psychiatrists for years.

The difference is that the clients finally learned that the switch was inside of them all along. God was trying to tell them that they had control over that from the beginning. God was not holding back. He'd already given them what they needed. When they learned how to focus on believing the truth and on being calm, their state changed quite well.

Your state responds relatively quickly to any change in the focus of your thoughts. Your thoughts include your perceptions, beliefs, interpretations, intentions, and self-talk. Self-talk is the conversation going on inside of your head at any given moment. Any change in the focus of your thoughts will begin to create a change in some aspect of your state. The idea is to make sure that the process is moving in the direction you desire, otherwise, the tendency will be to revert to the old way of doing things.

How you see yourself, the world, and God may indicate the need for a lens change.

Personal Responsibility

> "Man does not control his own fate. The women in his life do that for him."
>
> Groucho Marx, American comedian, writer, stage, film, radio, and televisión star

Since the switch is inside of us and something clearly in your and my control, it's essential that each of us take personal responsibility for our state. When you blame others and circumstances, you're revealing your belief that your locus of control is external, while the reality is your switch resides in no one but you.

Sometimes you'll meet people who believe that your switch is in them. They think that they're responsible for how you feel. They're sweet, kind people. They want others to be happy. They've come to believe – falsely – that they're responsible for other's happiness. Some have labeled this type of person pleasers or co-dependents. Most of us have some pleaser or co-dependent in us to some extent.

Pleasers eventually base their life on trying to please others and do whatever others want in the vain attempt to "make" them happy. They'll do so to their detriment, even to the point of being violated and chronically miserable and depressed. Maybe you know someone like that. Perhaps you are someone like that. The tribe of pleasers has many members, and they tend to vacillate back and forth between guilt and resentment. They tend to believe others must change in order for them to feel and be better. The solution to being a pleaser is to embrace the truth that only you are responsible for how you feel and others are responsible for their feelings.

Another type of external locus person believes that you are responsible for how they feel. They refuse to be accountable for their own stuff. As you might guess, the second type drifts toward personalities who feel responsible for others. It only makes sense. The second type who want to hold you accountable tends to be abusers and controllers. They blame and manipulate with guilt. Those with addictions commonly have a belief on some level that others are responsible for how they feel. The best way to be around and deal with this type of person is to be crystal clear within yourself that each of you are only responsible for yourselves.

Victim Versus Victor

> "I'd rather be a victor than a victim."
>
> Robert Kiyosaki, American businessman and author

There's a ton written about the difference between a victim mindset and a victor mindset. Primarily, a victim blames others and fails to take personal responsibility for their thoughts, feelings, and behavior. Victims are focused on what they're against, feels sorry for themselves and expects others to make them change.

It's interesting that the word "victim," comes from the Latin word "victima," denoting the person or creature killed as a religious sacrifice to appease the gods. That's not who any of us want to be, yet that's who how some of us act. If you're going to remain a victim, it might be wise to invest in some asbestos underwear. Leaving the victim identity behind can be pretty uncomfortable at first. Victims intensely dislike discomfort. They also seem to disdain personal responsibility.

A victor takes personal responsibility for their thoughts, feelings, and behavior. They take responsibility for their results. They're focused on what they're for. They know it's up to them, and they *will* find a way. Only those with a victor mindset will eventually achieve the goals they've set out to accomplish on a consistent basis. They'll also have a much better time on the journey than their victim counterparts. Be a victor.

Victor or Abuser

> "Evil requires the sanction of the victim."
>
> Ayn Rand, Russian-American novelist, philosopher, playwright and screenwriter

Many people confuse a victor with an abuser. Nothing could be farther from the truth. An abuser is aggressive, not assertive. A victor is assertive, not aggressive.

In my next case study, you'll read about Celeste. In time she would discover that she had at least one belief telling her that to be a victor is in reality the same as being an abuser; however, that is inaccurate.

An aggressive person is one who is still operating from a victim mindset. They still work on the belief that other people are responsible for how they feel, what others think is less important than what they do, and the only way they believe they can be strong is by dominating others. Aggression and abusive behavior flow from a core emotion of fear. Those who are aggressive desperately fear loss and being out of control. The abuser uses force and manipulation to avoid feeling out of control. Regardless of how their actions result in a deteriorating outcome, they persist with what doesn't work.

The victor takes personal responsibility for their thoughts, feelings, and behavior, and in turn they give others the privilege of being personally responsible for their thoughts, feelings, and behavior. Victors realize that if they're focused and determined enough, they can have whatever they want or need in a way that works for both themselves and for others. They realize that they are interdependent with others, neither independent nor dependent on others. It's alright to have what they want and need and to have clear boundaries without any guilt. To have that, they must first answer the question about whether it is okay to be powerful.

Positive Versus Negative

> "Anyone can train to be a gladiator. What marks you out is having the mindset of a champion."
>
> Manu Bennett, actor

A person with a positive mindset focuses on the desired outcome. A person with a negative mindset focuses on what they're avoiding. It's not possible to be legitimately empowered when focused on an undesirable alternative. True empowerment only happens when you're focused on what is much better. A positive mindset takes responsibility for false, negative beliefs, and follows steps to transform them into real, high-quality replacements. Everything about your state flows from your mindset.

Case Study: Celeste

Celeste's mother has a history of being needy and calling on Celeste to take care of her. Her mother was unavailable when Celeste was little. Her mother had had several husbands, and some of them molested Celeste. Celeste has been in several relationships that have failed. Her mother still makes demands on her, decades later. If Celeste doesn't do what an abusive partner wants, or what her mother wants, she feels guilty. Sound familiar? It is to literally millions of women around the world.

The same thing happens if one of her kids places undue demands on her. Celeste is now middle-aged, and the stress is overwhelming. She feels anxious and depressed but can't seem to say no without horrible guilt. Eventually, Celeste uses anger to try to get others to back off of their demands, but she ultimately gives in and gives them what they want. However, after giving in, she's plagued with resentment. Her whole life has been one big pendulum swing between guilt and resentment.

Celeste sees herself as a victim. She sees herself as having been powerless to resist abuse as a young girl and now imagines herself powerless to do anything about her mother, partners, or kids. She feels blamed by them and she also blames them for how unsuccessful she is in life and how much of a mess her life has become.

It took Celeste a while to understand the principle of focusing on what she's for. Once she did, however, she began to apply it to her situation with her mother. She noticed her anxiety calm down and her sleep improve. The next question for Celeste to ask herself became if she didn't want to be a victim with her mother, what would she rather be. Does she want to continue to be the person who gets thrown onto the sacrificial altar? It must be a pretty cushy job based on how much energy she expends to stay in that job.

The opposite of a victim is a victor. What would a victor look like in Celeste's world? Just thinking about being a victor would probably bring up overwhelming guilt in Celeste. She would be concerned about how being strong would hurt so many people, and it would be all her fault. She has some belief transformation to achieve. This kind of thinking keeps thousands, if not millions, of people like Celeste in a no-win bind every moment of every day. It takes courage for them to break out. I've personally known hundreds who have broken out. It can happen.

CHAPTER FOUR
A FORCE MULTIPLIER

Your transformation begins with the innermost you, with your mindset. When your thoughts change, your emotions and actions change. Emotions and actions can cycle back around and amplify your thoughts and feelings, which can result in a spiral effect. The spiral could be either positive or negative, depending on the quality of your original thoughts, beliefs, and intention.

As Jesus said, if the tree is good the fruit will be good. Your tree also affects other people, the atmosphere, and the universe itself. It doesn't make you feel different or result in different behavior; it influences what could be called a spiritual effect.

Case Study: Sheila

> "Only I can change my life. No one can do it for me."
>
> Carol Burnett, American actress, comedian, singer and writer

Sheila was a young college girl with a bit of a problem.

The problem was that Sheila had been depressed for two years. It was pretty bad and getting worse. She was becoming suicidal and had lost all but one friend. That friend had just let her know that she was thinking of leaving, too. According to her friend, Sheila had been pushing people away for a long time. According to Sheila, they were all a bunch of jerks, anyway. Sheila was angry at everyone.

Apparently, two years earlier, the students and teacher in her favorite class stopped talking to her and stopped listening to her. They wouldn't even look at her. Sheila became hurt and angry. Hurt and anger lead to depression and an intensely dark, negative mindset.

Sheila learned about the *Pink Elephants and White Tigers* concept. She had read a book about the law of attraction and realized it was similar. Her understanding of the law of attraction was that what she sends out into the universe is what she gets back. Sheila learned that *Pink Elephants and White Tigers* is kind of like a mini law of attraction. Other people were responding to the little invisible signals that she was sending out. It dawned on her that how other people were treating her might be coming from her. She was eager to do something about it.

I carefully explained to Sheila that if she expected others to hate her, they could sense that and would treat her as if they hated her. Others would be perfectly okay with any expectation for them to hate her, or to love her. They were just waiting for subtle instructions from her.

Researchers have determined[20] that people tend to be naturally drawn toward others when their eyebrows are up and they have a smile on their face. In the same way, they tend to move away from people when their eyebrows are furrowed and they are not smiling or are frowning. It seems self-evident and not really worthy of a research study.

My assignment for Sheila was to go home and spend three to five minutes each evening in front of her mirror with her eyebrows up and a big smile on her face looking at herself. She was to do this every evening for at least five evenings. After practicing for a few days, I suggested that before she walked into the classroom, she should get her eyebrows up, put a big smile on her face, open the door and make direct eye contact with the first three people she saw. She did just that, and guess what happened? She reported that everyone began talking to her and smiling at her as if nothing had ever happened.

Within the next six weeks, Sheila reported having no depression at all. So, who was responsible for her depression and lack of friends? The short answer is that she was. When Sheila focused on the belief that no one liked or loved her, she non-verbally sent that message out to people around her. Remember, communication is only 15% verbal, but 85% non-verbal.

Other people had been picking up the subtle cue that they didn't like her or love her, that they, in fact, hated her. Somehow that got registered in their unconscious minds, and they responded in kind. They had no idea why they suddenly didn't like her. It was merely a response to a subtle and hypnotic suggestion.

When Sheila instead focused on the belief that everyone loved and liked her, that she expected to be loved and liked, their unconscious minds picked it up and they responded by thinking and acting on those feelings. In general, most people like to love someone. By pre-programming her own belief that everyone loves and likes her, Sheila also will unconsciously begin doing things that will maximize others loving and liking her. It's automatic.

Sheila was responsible for her problem. She was also responsible for the solution. Personal responsibility is essential if you want to change your life. What happened to Sheila is an excellent example of how a change of mindset changed her state, and how her changed state affected others around her. The effect on others around her then positively touched her.

Iatrogenesis

> "Think twice before you speak, because your words and influence will plant the seed of either success or failure in the mind of another."
>
> Napoleon Hill, American self-help author

Iatrogenesis is another powerful concept illustrating the point of Sheila's dilemma and solution. The first part of the word, "iatro" means, "other." The second part of the word, "genesis," means "to create."

As mentioned briefly in Chapter One, iatrogenesis means "brought forth by the healer," in essence created by someone else. It's used to refer to illness brought on in a patient by the physician.

By the 1960s, iatrogenesis was recognized as a common problem in the medical field. On one end of the continuum, there were hundreds of doctors whose patients routinely became worse and died. On the other end of the continuum, there was a group of hundreds of doctors whose patients – with the same diagnoses and general characteristics as the patients with the ineffective doctors – tended only to get better, survive and thrive.

Interviewing the doctors whose patients exhibited poor results indicated that they were doctors who practiced medicine by the book. If their medical journals said that a patient with a particular diagnosis would be dead in six weeks, then that's what they told their patient. The patient heard the prognosis, then faithfully complied with the prophecy and were dead right on schedule.

The doctors on the other side ignored the medical journals. They told their patients that their condition was not a problem and would respond well to treatment. The patients believed them. In statistically large percentages they overcame the odds. Many of them would heal and go on to live healthy lives.

Conversely, if iatrogenesis could result in illness and death, it could result in healing and life. The expectations and intentions of others can affect you for better or worse. Your expectations of them can change them for better or worse. So, **pay careful attention to what you're telling yourself about you. Pay careful attention to what you're thinking and saying about others.**

The Atmosphere

The atmosphere is the cushion of air that surrounds the earth. Depending on where you happen to be, the atmosphere might be humid or dry. It might be cold, warm, or hot. Even a building or a room can have its unique atmosphere. It can be cold, warm, or hot, humid or dry. It can also be friendly or hostile, safe or unsafe, orderly and in control, or out of control. The coherence of one person's state can affect the climate of others nearby.

Somewhere I read of a study done in the late 1980s and early 1990s. In this study, they worked with about 2,000 participants. A test was administered to determine the state of each participant at a specific point in time. Three people who tested as having a neutral state joined with a fourth person who was in a coherent emotional state, such as being angry, depressed, or happy. The four people were not allowed to look at each other or speak to each other for fifteen minutes.

At the end of the allotted time, each participant received a follow-up test. In every case, those who were neutral and grouped with an angry person became angry after fifteen minutes with the angry person. Those who were neutral and grouped with a depressed person became depressed after only fifteen minutes. Those who were neutral and grouped with a happy person interviewed as feeling happier after fifteen minutes.

The general conclusion was that those who are in a neutral, low coherence state tend to conform to those in a dominant emotional state.

Those in a dominant emotional state control the atmosphere. However, is it only the emotional state involved? Studies, such as by Martha K. McClintock, have shown that women in large organizations and the military will tend to eventually have their cycles around the same time as one another.[21] A phenomenon she calls, "Menstrual Synchrony." I suspect they're cycling in sync with the dominant female.

In 1665, Christiaan Huygens placed two pendulum clocks (grandfather clocks) in a room, wound them up and got them ticking. Within a short period of time they were both ticking in sync with one another.[22]

Emotion may be the most natural variable to observe, but remember, feelings are a byproduct of mindset and intention, whether positive or negative. Something is happening with the coherence of intention that seems to be affecting the atmosphere. Those in the most dominant, focused, and intentional state, tend to control the influence over others nearby.

A Personal Example

My wife and I discovered this truth several years ago. For a few years in a row, we hosted annual get-togethers with many family members. One particular person was a negative, disruptive person, so consequently the get-togethers were very unpleasant.

One year, about three months before the upcoming get together, my wife decided to clarify and focus her intention to see what would happen to the atmosphere. She focused her intention on the atmosphere as calm, peaceful, and loving. I supported her by concentrating my intention in the same way. We specifically prayed about it.

At the next get together, the disruptive person was uncharacteristically calm, quiet, and very well behaved. They even had a look of confusion on their face as if they weren't sure how to act. It all started from the inside out. The power of coherent intention created the desired atmosphere based on the principles that govern the spiritual and quantum universe.

A Force Multiplier

In her book *The Intention Experiment*,[23] Lynn MacTaggart describes the results of research on the effects on the atmosphere of society as a result of practicing Transcendental Meditation (TM).

On page 182, she reports that research indicates that if the square root of 1 percent of the population of an area practices TM-Sidhi (an advanced form of meditation), then, "conflict of any variety – the rate of murders, crime, drug abuse, even traffic accidents – goes down." She reports that twenty-two studies indicated a positive impact of what she calls the "Maharishi Effect" on crime levels. I believe that the research about TM illustrates the power of coherent, group intention.

Does this mean that only those who practice TM-Sidhi can influence their atmosphere? By no means.

Jesus said, "For where two or three are gathered in my name, there am I among them." Matthew 18:20, ESV.

Imagine you're in an empty room with about nine other people. You ask everyone to hit the wall with their shoulder at the count of three. You count to three and everyone hits the wall. Some are now rubbing their shoulders in pain. Ouch.

Next, you point to a specific point on a wall. This time you tell everyone that at the count of three, they should hit that point simultaneously. Now when you count to three and everyone converges at the same point, at the same time, they plow right through the wall.

The collective force of them all going to the same spot at the same time is enormous. It works the same way with group intention. If everyone is intending, believing, and praying with the same mind, intensely, at the same time, the atmosphere will bend in that direction. If you want to affect the atmosphere of a community, at the very least, get the square root of 1% of the population to agree, and it will happen.

The county in which I live is reported to have a population of 150,000. Applying the rule of thumb discovered by those who practice TM-Sidhi, a group of 39 like-minded individuals in a coherent agreement can change the atmosphere of the entire county. What would you like the atmosphere in your world to be? When you get a clear vision of that with a few other people, intend and pray with that in mind, it will likely manifest.

Systems Theory

Systems theory is a term out of a book entitled *General System Theory: Foundations, Development, Applications*.[24] It's a theory that accounts for how systems operate in biology, astronomy, physics, chemistry, and other scientific areas. The principle can be extended to the area of your life mentally, emotionally, and spiritually.

Even our solar system operates according to some definite laws. Each planet has its orbit around the sun. Everything will continue on course and unchanged forever. However, systems theory also says that if you change any part of the system, the rest of the system will automatically adapt to accommodate the change. For example, if the trajectory of Mars was to be critically altered by a collision with an asteroid, the orbits of the other planets would rearrange into a different pattern.

The same phenomenon happens in your mind, as well. Beliefs, perceptions, emotions, and actions tend to work together as a system. When you change one false view, the rest of the system has to adapt accordingly.

That can force the next false belief to the surface quickly. As each is dealt with appropriately, the overall system will profoundly and permanently alter for the better. In all my years of experience, I've known that process to only work in the direction of health. I've never seen it work against a person.

Quantum Faith

> "Faith will either get you the thing or the thing to get the thing."
>
> Bill Winston, American preacher, author, visionary leader and business entrepreneur

In a sense, doesn't this seem like what Jesus was talking about when He said that if we have faith the size of a grain of mustard seed, we can remove mountains and mulberry trees and have them transplanted into the ocean? If faith is a form of coherent belief and intention that is in agreement and alignment with the truth of God, then it seems that what Jesus is referring to is the same as what quantum physicists refer to.

Annette Capps wrote a short book on this very subject called *Quantum Faith*.[25] She describes how the discoveries in quantum physics over the last eighty years readily confirm everything that Jesus taught over two thousand years ago. If faith is agreeing with God with no doubt in our hearts, then even the quantum physicists agree that the mountain will obey you when you command it to move.

Of course, those physicists haven't been doing experiments with moving mountains. They've been targeting smaller things like photons and fruit flies. Quantum physicists have apparently discovered that subatomic particles respond to being observed by the scientist. They seem to behave one way if unobserved and another way if directly viewed. Authors such as Lynn MacTaggart and Gregg Braden[26] have reported in great detail about the significant discoveries made by quantum physicists and how they relate to our everyday lives. Not only does the coherent intention of your thoughts influence how you feel, it affects the area around you, including how others feel and behave.

Sure, it's a much smaller scale than moving mountains, but a tiny thought can grow into something that will eventually change your life for either good or bad. That's a lot of power each of us has. It's even more significant when we link to others with like mind and move in the same direction. No wonder that one of the enemy's chief strategies is to divide us to conquer us. If we can be influenced to be lethargic, at odds with one another, powerless and incoherent, we are ineffective.

Even if there isn't an enemy trying to divide and control the rest of us, the quality of our lives is directly affected by our level of coherent intention, or the lack thereof. The more neutral an individual or group mind is, the more vulnerable it is to drifting in a negative direction. All it would take is a small handful of coherent, negatively focused others to interfere with a life worth living.

If you're a person of faith, it's time to realize how powerful your faith is. Quantum physics is repeatedly confirming a Biblical fact scientifically. Your faith affects the fabric of both the spiritual and physical worlds. It's time to learn how to have faith without doubt and team up with other like-minded individuals to create the world God is calling you to create.

If you're not a person of faith, it's time to wake up and discover how important faith is. Clear away the illusion that you've thought the world is. Tune into the truth about the lessons from quantum physics, especially in the context of what Jesus has taught.

PART TWO
THE POWER

CHAPTER FIVE
TOOLS OF THE TRADE

In the first three chapters, I mentioned one or two tools that can be used to improve the quality of your mindset, intention, and coherence level.

In this chapter, I will focus on the tools I've found to be the most powerful and helpful for me. They're also the tools that others whom I've trained over the years report back as being their favorites.

Please keep in mind that you might be able to learn these tools from others. They may have some variations that seem to be pretty cool, but not everyone teaches these the same. I suggest that you learn the basics, read up on other variations, but most importantly, practice. Remember, that's how you get to Carnegie Hall; practice, practice, practice. With some coached practice you can get pretty good at using these tools and decide how you'd like to customize them with your own, personal variations.

It's my bias to keep things as simple as possible. I like them to be clear, simple, and effective, so if you're not getting good results from one or more of these, let me know, and we can troubleshoot it together.

Tool One: Mental Rehearsal

Mental rehearsal is exactly what it sounds like – rehearsing something in your mind.

Mental rehearsal is an incredibly powerful tool for your self-improvement toolbox, if used correctly. What I mean by that is it's a tool that everyone already has in their toolbox. In fact, pretty much every human being uses mental rehearsal every day, even though most people tell me they've never heard of it. Some people call it visualization or creative visualization, but the problem with that is some people are more auditory or tactile and don't really visualize anything.

You can mentally rehearse anything without being able to visualize. The mental part simply means the mind is purposefully involved in choosing how and what you rehearse. Research shows that there's a certain point where the mind can't tell the difference between thinking about doing something and actually doing it. That's the power behind mental rehearsal.

Lynn MacTaggart tells about experiments run by Guang Yue, an exercise psychologist at Cleveland Clinic Foundation in Ohio and a similar experiment by Dr. David Smith at Chester College in 1997. A group of athletes who wanted to improve their athletic performance were split into a control group and an experiment group. The control group were given a work out plan to follow at a gym on a regular basis. The experiment group was given the same regimen that they were to perform in their mind while sitting in an easy chair at home.

Both groups faithfully performed their plan for several weeks. At the end of the experiment, those who had only practiced in their mind showed an improvement in muscle size and strength of between 13.5% to 16% compared to 30% with those who actually used the gym.[27]

How Does It Apply in Your Life?

Mental rehearsal can be used to improve pretty much any skill or area of your life. Here are just a few examples:

- Programming yourself to go to sleep at a certain time;
- Programming yourself to awaken at a certain time;
- Programming yourself to overcome insomnia;
- Feeling calm and confident in uncertain situations;
- Improving your performance of a musical instrument or vocal skills;
- Improving your sports performance;
- Improving your business success;
- Improving your people skills.

Mental rehearsal can also be used to create an improved response to any difficult circumstance or trigger such as responding more proactively to someone who sets you off like a toxic person, coworker, or spouse, and handling dangerous or frustrating situations like being cut off in traffic or handling critical incidents.

Those are just a few examples, but there are thousands.

How I Learned About and Used Mental Rehearsal

I first heard of mental rehearsal when I was in my mid-teens in high school. My favorite geology teacher had a substitute one day who spent the entire class telling us about mental rehearsal.

He told us that if we had some area in life where we wanted improvement, such as a sport activity, or as a musician, we could make a big difference by creating a short video clip in our mind. He explained that if we created a thirty to sixty second video clip in our mind of performing the task exactly the way we want to perform it and played it 8-10 or more times a day, around two weeks later, we would be performing that task exactly as we'd rehearsed it.

The idea was to include as many details in the video clip as we could, such as sounds, smells, textures, emotions (feeling the way we would want to feel), other people's reactions and so forth. For this reason, some refer to it as *Multi-Sensory Mental Rehearsal*. Create a brief scenario of exactly how you want to handle any particular situation. Play it 8-10 or more times per day in your mind. Don't change anything. Only work on one change at a time until the new behavior is automated.

It was one of the most interesting classes I can remember in high school. The idea of mental rehearsal made a lot of sense to me. I didn't think much more about it until I was nineteen. By that time, I'd counted nearly two dozen times that I had locked my keys in my pickup truck. I even kept a coat hanger wrapped around the frame of the truck to be able to break back in, but that habit was beginning to tear the weather stripping on the door, which was not good.

It occurred to me to try the mental rehearsal I'd been taught by the teacher. So, I created a short video segment in my mind of pulling into the college parking lot, parking the truck, turning the ignition off, putting the keys into my pocket, opening the door, locking the door, picking up my books, exiting the truck and closing the door. I focused on feeling the steering wheel, hearing the sound of the truck, feeling the keys in my hand. I played it over and over more than ten times a day.

About ten days later I pulled into the parking space at the college, turned the ignition off, opened the door, locked the door and grabbed my books. I thought I'd forgotten to put the keys in my pocket, so I reached for them. No keys. I checked under the seat and on the floor. No keys. I checked in my pocket. There they were! I had absolutely no memory of putting them into my pocket.

At the same age, I had an auto route delivering the morning newspaper. It was a one hundred square mile route delivering over seven hundred papers a day.

I had to get up at 2AM to be at the station on time in order to have all the papers delivered timely, but my alarm clock didn't always work correctly. A couple of times I came close to losing my job. The thought of using mental rehearsal came to mind. It sure worked with my keys.

I created a short video of being deeply asleep and suddenly awaking at 2AM. Again, I imagined as many sensory experiences as I could, such as the feel of the pillow and sheets, the feeling of being relaxed, and so on. I played the video in my head about 10-15 times per day.

About a week later, I was laying on my back completely asleep. Suddenly, I shot up in a seated position as if startled awake. It was very disorienting. I looked at the clock, and it said, "2:01AM." I climbed out of bed and went to deliver my papers. On some level, it seemed like that could be a fluke. The next morning, I was deeply asleep and laying on my side, facing the alarm clock. My eyes suddenly opened and I looked at the clock. It said, "1:59AM." I climbed out of bed and went to deliver my papers.

For the next 18 months, I never slept past 2:01AM. It took me the use of mental rehearsal to train myself to sleep past 2AM after I quit that job.

Since then, I've used mental rehearsal thousands of times. In my twenties, I used mental rehearsal several times to have a specific type of dream that I wanted to have, like flying. I would create the scenario I'd like to have and play the video in my head several times a day. Within two weeks, I would have that dream. I also used it to reprocess disturbing dreams, particularly if they were repetitive. After imagining a different turning point in the sequence, it would eventually shift and the dream wouldn't come back.

How Can It Work for You?

The vitally important point is not only how well mental rehearsal worked for me and can work for you, but how everyone uses it every day. Whatever way that you notice that you respond to certain situations is a result of how you've been mentally rehearsing. It's usually negative for most people.

If you do a little inventory, you'll probably realize that you mentally rehearse having toxic responses to some people. Then, when certain situations occur, you react exactly the way you've imagined, and you reinforce your negative reaction by telling yourself that you knew precisely what was going to happen. Change what and how you rehearse and eventually you'll respond entirely differently. The big question to answer for yourself is how you would like to respond.

Some important things to keep in mind when practicing mental rehearsal are:

- Be clear exactly how you'd like to perform the task that you're about to rehearse.
- Keep it simple.
- Be clear about how you desire to feel when the event occurs.
- Practice the rehearsal a minimum of ten times per day.
- When you practice it, really mean it.
- Once you've created what you want in your rehearsal, don't change anything. If you alter something, you're essentially starting over.
- Work on one thing at a time until you get good at it.

What If I Can't See Images?

Some people say that they're incapable of creating visual images in their mind. If that's the case for you, it probably means you're not a visual person. Your representational system may be more auditory or tactile (touch). However, all is not lost. Some alternatives for you have the same benefit. The first is what is called a creative narrative, discussed in the next section.

It's also believed that if you get your body involved in acting out the rehearsal, you'll amp up the effectiveness even more. That would be the virtual equivalent of being in a simulator such as what pilots use to learn to fly in all sorts of adverse conditions. How you set up and practice your rehearsal is how you'll show up when the event occurs.

Where in My Life Can I Use it?

Mental rehearsal is applicable to a wide range of areas in your life. It can be used to change your behavior, your emotional responses, to calm you down, and to increase your motivation. In fact, it's one of the healthiest forms of self-motivation I've ever experienced or taught.

Case Study: Sierra

When you think over your life, ask yourself how it is that you typically get yourself motivated. If you're like most people, you use some variation of the shame approach, which means you tend to beat yourself up or put yourself down in an attempt to motivate yourself, when the truth is shaming yourself increases internal stress and eventually destroys your performance.

It may have worked for a while when you were younger, like waiting until Friday night to do a 30-page term paper due Monday morning even though you had three months to work on it. Maybe you got an 'A' that time and thought you'd discovered that the secret to life is procrastination. Intuitively you may have realized that when you were desperate enough, you'd got it done. However, continuing to procrastinate as your preferred method of motivation will wear on you. It will eventually affect your health, your relationships, and it will neutralize your effectiveness.

Consider what happened to Sierra a few years ago and how mental rehearsal profoundly helped her after her shame nearly killed her. Sierra was in her late forties and had been profoundly depressed for five years. A good detective would be asking what happened five years ago, and that's exactly what I asked her.

Five years before, she and her family moved into their new home. They stacked all the boxes in in such a way that the family could barely walk from one room to another. She committed to her family that she would unpack the boxes.

The boxes never got unpacked.

Sierra fell into a deep depression and just became withdrawn. Eventually, her family got frustrated and insisted she complete what she agreed to do. I asked her if she knew what was in the boxes. She assured me she knew the exact contents of each box.

I explained mental rehearsal carefully to her. I coached her to imagine taking down one box. She imagined taking one item at a time out of the box and putting it away as if she were doing it in real time. After unpacking the box in her mind, I asked her if she was up to an assignment. She said she was. I requested that she go home, take that box down and put only one item away before our next visit. She agreed.

At Sierra's next visit, I asked how it went. She said the dining room was completely cleared out. She reported that after she put one item away, she automatically put another, then another away. Within a few hours, the boxes were empty, and the dining room cleared. Since the moment the last box was removed, she had no more depression. It was gone.

Pushing and shaming herself resulted in her trying to force a square peg into a round hole. It was a self-defeating form of motivation. Imagining it with mental rehearsal programmed her mind to do what she wanted all along. Her mind robotically followed the instructions it was given.

How mental rehearsal can apply to other areas:

- Business:
  It can help with being relaxed and more effective when giving presentations, it is useful for reducing daily stress, and it is useful to imagine what needs to be done today and successfully accomplishing it. Mental rehearsal can also be used to dissolve distractions, obstacles, troubling thoughts, or beliefs.

- Marriage:
  With mental rehearsal, you can train yourself to have a calm response to toxic transactions, to be more skillful in communicating, especially listening, and to build up healthy love and feelings of affection after the honeymoon effect has worn off.

- Music:
  Mental rehearsal can be used to train yourself to play those problematic segments flawlessly and automatically. Most musicians are taught mental rehearsal early in their schooling even though that term is new to them. They're usually surprised to hear that they can transfer that skill to other areas of life.

- Sports:
  Focus on a specific action that you want to improve. For example, in baseball, you might be focusing on hitting a particular pitch or catching a specific type of ball scenario. Professional players spend millions of dollars per year hiring coaches who can train them in Mental Rehearsal.

- Personal:
  Mental rehearsal can be useful for remembering appointments, remembering to take things home, changing responses to interpretations and beliefs, eating better, overcoming compulsions, stress reduction, motivation, and sleep.

Tool Two: The Creative Narrative

The creative narrative is a variation of mental rehearsal. Mental rehearsal and the creative narrative work powerfully together.

What can you do if you have a tough time with having an imagination as some do? For that, you can apply a creative narrative. It's pretty much the same process as mental rehearsal, except that you write down on paper a clear description of what you want in your mental rehearsal. It's worth taking the time to write it down.

Using your best writing hand engages your tactile representational system. If you're a more tactile person, the information will be more readily received and processed by your mind. Even if you're not dominantly tactile, it's at least adding one more representational channel to support the acceptance of the new program.

Write everything down in reasonable detail. Don't hold back or worry if it takes ten pages. Include everything that you would if you were using only your imagination. After writing it down, read it out loud 10-20 times a day. Read it slowly and with meaning. Saying it out loud uses your auditory representational system. It's possible that you could be either primarily or secondarily auditory. It can also be helpful to record yourself saying it and then play back the recording several times a day. Listen to it as you drive from one place to another, during a short break in between tasks, and just before going to sleep at night.

If you're able to include all three representational systems – imagination, tactile, and auditory – you're getting the maximum influence of input. Keep it up regularly until you notice that what you're targeting changes in the desired direction.

Tool Three: Grounding and Centering

If you've attended any self-improvement training in the last thirty years, it's very likely you've seen some form of grounding and centering demonstrated. There are a few different variations that are highly applicable to personal change and growth. Any area of your life in which you'd like to respond to stress calmly is a perfect place to use grounding and centering.

The skill of grounding and centering was initially taught as a core part of Aikido training. Aikido is a martial art created by Morihei Ueshiba over a hundred years ago. When used correctly, the Aikido practitioner enters a state where their chi energy focuses on an area just below the belly button. They also practice being grounded to the earth, as if roots are growing from their feet into the ground. In a grounded and centered state, the practitioner is a formidable force with which to reckon. They are calm, precisely focused, unusually aware of details in their environment, highly creative, very difficult to move, and able to leverage the power of punches and kicks much more potently than when out of center.

As a teenager, I was in a karate class in which we practiced full contact karate. The instructor had formerly been the instructor for the Korean National Police. He was quite no-nonsense and traditional. As a white belt, I would get onto the mat against the higher belts and get smacked around pretty good. They were blindingly fast!

The instructor called me aside and carefully taught me how to ground and center. He told me to practice several times a day and continue regularly. I practiced and practiced. It took about two weeks to get the hang of it.

When I went back to the mat and entered a calm, centered and grounded state, it was like a form of self-hypnosis. I was surprised to learn that I could sense a split second before my opponent was going to punch or kick. Faster than I could think on a conscious level, I was blocking and punching as blindingly fast as they were. It was like I was sitting in a comfortable chair watching it on television. In one match I was kicked in the chest by my opponent. I responded by flipping over and landing on my feet. Me, a guy who had no gymnastic ability!

The training I practiced over the years to be good at grounding and centering has helped me with hiking in dangerous terrain. It's also supported me to be calm, focused, and highly creative in response to extremely stressful situations and people. Once you've learned how to ground and center, the main idea is to allow any and all negative forces and factors to pass through you as if you're a ghost. You're non-corporeal.

If someone says something hurtful, it's common for most people to let the hurtful comment wound them. It's like they shot an arrow and it stuck somewhere in the other person's body. When you're in a grounded and centered state, you'll tend to allow the arrow to pass through you, off the horizon, and into outer space. There's nowhere in you for it to stick.

Imagine that you and I are standing next to a waterfall. It's a beautiful day. In my hand, I have a compound bow and a razor-sharp tipped arrow. I string my arrow, draw the bow, aim at the waterfall, and release. The arrow makes its way through the waterfall. Does the arrow mess up the waterfall's day? Unlikely. There will be a blip, and the arrow will be gone. As far as the waterfall is concerned, the arrow is a non-event.

What if the painful arrows from life and other people were like that for you? They pass right through you, off the horizon, into outer space, nothing more than a momentary blip. Would that be a game changer? It indeed has been for me and many, many others.

Imagine you're driving around town on any old day. You've practiced being grounded and centered so much it's pretty automatic for you to be there. Someone suddenly pulls in front of you, honks, and flips you off. Being grounded and centered, you allow it to pass through you easily. Automatically you follow through with how you've mentally rehearsed handling this situation. Within seconds, the event is over, and you move on comfortably with your day, perhaps mumbling a quick prayer for the impulsive driver who is apparently uncentered.

Imagine you're in an uncomfortable discussion with your spouse. It's heating up. You give yourself a cue to become grounded and centered. After practicing enough times, shifting into a grounded and centered state is easy. Right on schedule, your spouse says that thing that has upset you in the past. This time it passes through you. It's a non-event. With no conscious thought, you follow through with how you've mentally rehearsed this situation.

The same principles apply to making more money. Suppose your plan for increasing your income involves laying some groundwork that'll take a lot of time, energy, and focus before it ever pays off. There could easily be some psychological and emotional resistance, such as impatience. Being grounded and centered could help you glide through that otherwise tough time like skinny dipping in a cool lake. Allow the impatience to merely pass through you.

It takes practice. The more you practice, the better you become. It's a dynamic combination to include grounding and centering with your mental rehearsal. Clarify how you want your rehearsal to go, then practice your mental rehearsal in a grounded and centered state. At the same time, imagine that you're entirely grounded and centered in your imagery. What I and others have found is that you'll tend to go automatically into a grounded and centered state when your targeted event occurs, just as you've rehearsed.

Tool Four: Self Hypnosis

A hypnotist uses carefully worded language to elicit a hypnotic response from a subject, or a client. Hypnosis is nothing more than one person making a series of carefully worded suggestions to another. The client's responsiveness to suggestions indicates the depth of their hypnotic state. Some unusually powerful results can happen with a sufficiently responsive client. Rather than going to someone else to hypnotize you, why not be the one to give yourself the suggestions? After all, that's really the purpose of *Pink Elephants and White Tigers*.

You can learn to do self-hypnosis by following a tutorial on YouTube or reading about it in a book. The effect is similar to the combination of mental rehearsal with grounding and centering, anyway.

Tool Five: Energy Psychology

There are hundreds of different techniques around that use what is now called energy psychology, which is the blend of what is taught and believed in acupuncture with some Western thought added. Out of the hundreds of techniques using energy psychology, the two that are the most applicable to our discussion are Emotional Freedom Technique (EFT) and Psych K as mentioned earlier. Some refer to EFT simply as "Tapping."

EFT is simple to learn and can quickly shift you out of a negative emotion. It involves tapping on various meridian points on your body while repeating a word or phrase. You can learn EFT for free by visiting www.emofree.com. Dr. Gary Craig, the man who developed EFT, has resources for learning how to use and apply it to a variety of life issues.

Psych K was developed in 1988 by Robert M. Williams, M.A. It's a technique that's specifically used to change self-limiting beliefs in the deep part of the mind, from the inside out. Although you can learn to be a Psych K provider, it may be more useful to go online and find a qualified Psych K practitioner to help you shift any self-limiting beliefs that have been difficult for you to change any other way.

I have personal experience with at least a half-dozen variations of energy psychology. From my experience, EFT and Psych K are the simplest and most effective. They're also available for you to learn and use without having to have a license or expensive training, unlike some of the other techniques require. Energy psychology is a simple, yet powerful tool. I've used energy psychology techniques for years and found them to be transformational for both myself and clients. Many others I've met have told me they've used energy psychology techniques to assist in transforming their lives, too.

Energy psychology takes practice. Once you've learned any of the techniques, they're yours to use whenever you like. They're portable, and they fit nicely in your back pocket or left shoe.

Tool Six: The Intention Question[28]

A question is just a question, is it not? Maybe, but not all questions are created equal. Some are downright powerful.

Did you know that in the area of communication, asking a question is a listening skill? In reality, it's the most abused communication skill people use. I teach my clients the number one reason to ask a question is to understand the speaker to the speaker's satisfaction. Tragically, that is most certainly not the reason most people ask questions.

The second most appropriate reason to ask a question is to get information to have an optimal outcome. In teaching communication skills, it's often said that it's not what question you're asking, but it's how you're asking it. Asking 'what' is important, but 'how' can be even more critical.

When asking a question of another person, be extremely clear about what your goal is. If it's to understand them accurately, they'll be thrilled. It's so sweet to have someone genuinely desire to understand. Ask the "how" question in an open, caring style. Rather than asking if their favorite color is purple, instead ask what is their favorite color.

Research About Questions

When I was in my undergraduate program, I recall reading that somehow researchers determined that when the human mind receives a question, it never stops looking for an answer – ever. They also determined that when the mind considers a question, it researches the answer at a rate of thirty times per second. I have no idea what method the researchers used to determine that, but it's what they reported.

I decided to test their results. I formed straightforward questions that I wanted to know the answer to and wrote them down. Sure enough, within a few seconds, to a few days, I'd have the answer.

What's an Intention Question?

An intention is the coherent focus and aim of your mind, something particular. An intention question is a highly focused question about which you want a specific answer. That question is then addressed to your unconscious mind. Immediately, your unconscious mind will begin looking for an answer. Hopefully, you're a good listener, because when the answer appears, it'll be clear. If you're a poor listener, you'll miss it.

An example of the intention question is "What is the simplest and most effective way that I can (insert problem you want or need solved)?"

It's been common for me and many of my clients to have a crystal-clear answer appear in my mind within seconds or minutes of asking the question or writing it down.

Mother-in-law's Fluorescent Light Fixture

A few years back I was faced with the dilemma of fixing my mother-in-law's old fluorescent lighting in her kitchen. The ballast was over thirty years old, and the replacement was half the size with twice as many wires.

The new ballast came with detailed instructions, but for hooking it up to a modern light fixture, not an older one. After hours of fiddling with it, I couldn't get the fixture to work, so I wrote down on a piece of paper the question of how I could wire it to ensure that it would work.

Nothing happened for the first two days and two nights. I re-read the question each night before bed. Three nights later, I awakened at 2AM with a clear image of how to wire the ballast. The next morning I went to her kitchen as early as I could, wired it the way I'd seen it in my mind, and it worked perfectly. Apparently, when asked the question, my mind began working on a solution immediately. It was entirely outside my conscious awareness.

That's incredible power!

I recall researchers also said that the human mind is capable of thinking on seven independently different tracks, plus or minus two, simultaneously. Wow! Your unconscious mind is created in the image of God Who is the Creator. That means you're designed with creative ability. When given a chance, that creative ability can come up with some fantastic solutions to overcoming any obstacles.

Be aware that you may not like the answer, but it probably will work. Make sure to phrase the question in a simple, clean form.

Don't write your questions including "and," "but," or long run-on questions. Just write a nice simple question that gets to the point. Some examples of clear intention questions would be:

- "How can this ballast be wired to allow the lights to work?" Or,
- "How can I come up with $5,000 within the next 30 days?" Or,
- "What's the best strategy for me to overcome this obstacle?"

The intention question is one of your most potent obstacle overcoming and problem-solving tools. Use it regularly. In the final analysis, it boils down to the basics. It's about how you respond to the obstacle and how you approach it that makes all the difference.

Tool Seven: Body Proclamation[29]

Stacy had been in one form of counseling or another for many years before she saw me as had so many other clients with whom I'd worked. She had a long-term anxiety problem, and no one had ever been able to help her entirely. Stacy's story was similar to hundreds I'd heard before. A pattern of anxiety from early in life continued to get worse over time, while a long trail of helping professionals resulted in little or no improvement over an extended period.

During her first few visits, I carefully explained the concept of *Pink Elephants and White Tigers* and how to focus on what she was for. It was hard for her to understand because of her overexposure to conventional therapy. A few visits later, she came in clearly shaken and visibly agitated. She insisted that she wanted to spend the session talking about what the root of her anxiety might be.

I respectfully declined to do that, pointing out that if it hadn't helped over the last several dozen mental health professionals, it was unlikely to help now.

Stacy asked what I would have her do differently. I asked her if she'd be willing to do a little exercise and she agreed.

I asked her how she would prefer to feel. She was a little confused at first, but after I clarified my question, she thought and finally settled on feeling calm. I explained she would need to repeat after me what I said as authentically as possible. She agreed.

To start, I asked her to say, "My toes feel calm." She repeated that. From there it was, "My ankles feel calm, my calves feel calm," and so on. We included internal organs and continued up through the top of her head.

Afterward, I asked her to tell me how she felt. She paused and reflected on her state. She said she had never experienced anything like this in her entire life. She had no anxiety and felt almost entirely calm. The whole process took less than two minutes. She reported later that the calm state lasted for the next five days.

Body proclamation combines focusing on what you're for with telling your body how you'd like to feel. Your unconscious mind is waiting for instructions and is more than happy to comply. Many clients have used this technique. The only time it doesn't work one hundred percent is for those who are getting some secondary benefit from their anxiety. They'd like to keep their anxiety.

Check out Appendix C for a Step-By-Step description of how to do Body Proclamation.

CHAPTER SIX
FINDING YOUR ZONE: WHERE THE LIFE WORTH LIVING HAPPENS

The Stress/Performance Curve

This part of the book can change your life even if the first part slipped past you as if you were Teflon-coated. It was a life changer for me and has been for many others I've met and taught.

You've probably heard about something called, "The Normal Curve." It's what statistics teachers teach and what your teacher in high school may have used to determine whether you flunked or graduated.

There's another curve that you may not have heard about, and that one is called "The Yerkes-Dodson Curve." It's also known as the "Stress/Performance Curve." I first learned about it in my undergraduate program. When I saw and understood it, I realized it was a game changer.

Here's what the curve looks like:

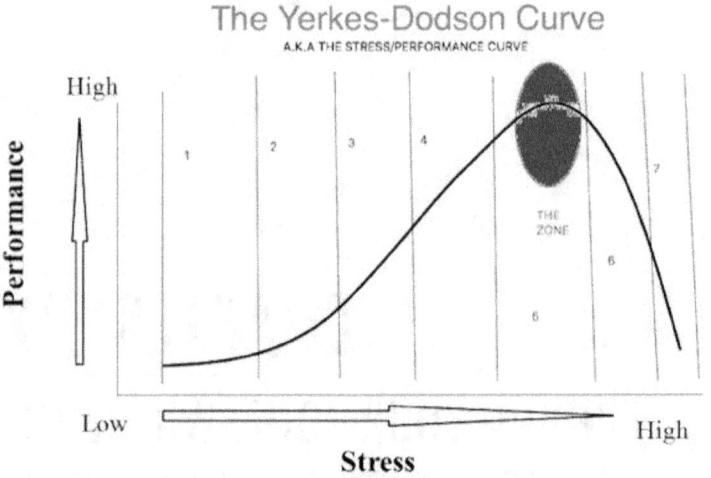

Think of it as a map in a mall with the "You Are Here" reference point that will also help you know how to get where you want to be.

The vertical axis on the left represents performance. Performance is what you do when responding to the demands of life to survive and thrive, or not. The bottom, left side of the axis is zero, meaning you're doing nothing. It goes up vertically from there. When performance is low, and stress is low, you'd tend to feel bored and maybe even antsy. There's a drive in you to increase your arousal.

The horizontal axis on the bottom represents stress. Stress is the demands of life, including the good, the bad, and everything else, whether internal or external stressors. The far-left side of the horizontal axis represents zero stress. It increases as the line travels to the right. As stress increases, performance increases. It increases slowly at first, like an aircraft doing its ground role on take-off.

Segments 1, 2, 3, and 4 represent the exponential increase in performance as stress increases. Each division has its own set of symptoms such as boredom or excitement. Your own response set significantly determines your performance.

Remember, your response to stress is something you can learn to re-adjust. It's possible to learn to adjust your response set until you can experience significantly more stressful situations with a fraction of the stress response. When stress continues to increase, performance continues to improve; that is, until, it reaches the peak of the curve.

On some intuitive level, we all know that as stress increases, so does performance. If you're not getting enough done, you tend to work harder. If working harder doesn't pay off enough, then you tend to beat yourself up. You call yourself names and shame yourself. Shaming yourself increases stress and increases performance. It works alright between the low side of the curve and the peak on the left side. It works against you on the right side of the summit.

If stress continues beyond the peak, then performance drops off, slowly at first, then it accelerates. Eventually, the curve abruptly ends. At that point, the person, or animal, dies. Their body can take no more stress. Death is usually due to organicity, which is the idea that when stress reaches a critical level, the weakest organ fails first.

The Zone

The peak is the sweet spot. It's where there's an ideal balance between the demands of life and your ability to perform. Athletes and business people call it "The Zone."

The Zone is where each person performs at their own, personal best. It's the home of the life worth living. Believe it or not, you've probably been in and out of your zone now and then in your life. It was during one of those times that you felt more fully alive, energized, engaged, and productive. It was great! Unfortunately, it didn't last long.

Since you didn't know where The Zone was, let alone how you got there or how to get back, you overshot and went to the right side of the curve. Overshooting happened most likely because you continued to motivate yourself using shame. It's like using a hammer, for every type of job you have to do.

As Kaplan's Law of the Instrument[30] indicates, "Give a boy a hammer and everything he meets has to be pounded."

The right side of the curve, such as areas 6 and 7, is what I call the "dark side." It's where stress symptoms show up. Symptoms are mild at first, such as short-term memory loss, difficulty concentrating, muscle tension, and irritability. Unfortunately, most of us don't realize what's going on and we walk farther into the dark side. Stress symptoms increase exponentially.

Moderate to severe symptoms are anxiety, panic, depression, addictions, heart attacks, cancer, strokes, ulcers, and more. Without knowing what they're doing, even applying a few stress reducers, most people hang out between area 6 and 7, even on a good day. If nothing is done to reduce stress, you die. That's the point where the curve ends.

The idea is for you to learn exactly where The Zone is from where you are now, make your way there, and learn to stay there. To do that, you'll need to replace the old, shame-based form of motivation with something much more pro-active. It will have to involve self-love, self-encouragement, and the willingness to include rest and trust in God. Also recall that mental rehearsal is one, such tool. Being focused on practicing positive self-talk and positive intention are powerful motivators to get you moving in the right direction.

There's a very cool conceptual tool developed in the early 1990s that can tell you how far away you are from The Zone and which direction you need to go to get there. It's an assessment tool that you can use as a sort of compass to find your way. It's called "The Wheel of Life."

The Wheel of Life[31]

The Wheel of Life assesses the ten major areas of each person's life based on a 1-10 scale of balance and fulfillment. In one circular graph you can get a snapshot of what's working and what isn't.

Imagine you're driving around in life in a vehicle with ten, large tires. Some of the tires have plenty of air in them, some are partially inflated, and some are flat. When these ten areas are at an eight to a ten, then your life has balance, and you're pretty much in The Zone. If one or more of them are less than an 8, it's like driving down the road with one or more flat tires.

Filling the chart out is relatively simple. Ask yourself how you're doing in each area on a 1 to 10 scale. Be honest. Mark the area accordingly. Any area that's not a ten is an area that has a gap requiring some attention.

What are your goals for those areas? What plan can you create to get to a ten in each of those? Hire a coach to walk with you to close those gaps, when you seem to be stuck or holding back. You can use the principle and strategies described in this book to close the gap in each area so you can reach a 10.

Here's the Wheel of Life.

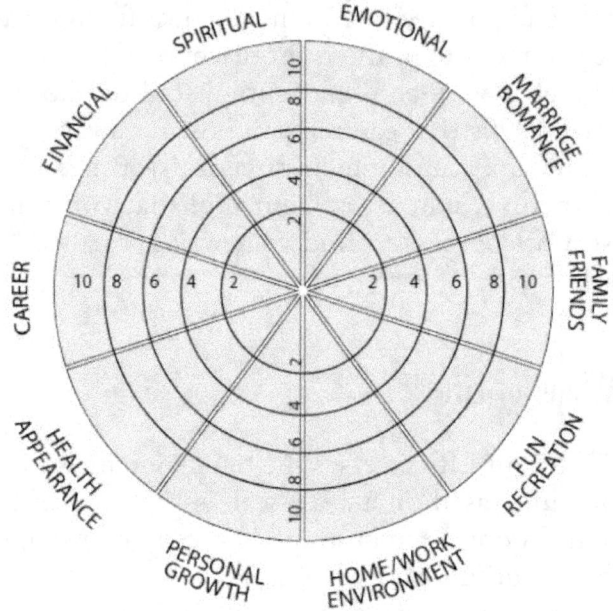

Using the Wheel of Life and symptoms that tell you which side of the curve you're on gives you a pretty accurate idea of where you are in relationship to your Zone.

When you use what's been taught in this book since Chapter 1 and apply it to each area of the Wheel of Life, you can make your way to The Zone and increase the time that you occupy that space. It's possible to be in and out of the ZONE several times per day, meaning that you can get back there whenever you're ready.

Which areas of The Wheel of Life need some loving-kind attention to get you there? Which tools appeal to you the most that you'd like to try out?

CHAPTER SEVEN
BULLDOZE THE BARRICADES: MAKING EASY WORK OF OBSTACLES

"Very often a change of self is needed more than a change of scene."

Arthur Christopher Benson, English essayist, poet, author and academic

What Obstacle?

When you're focused on what you're against, resistance is inevitable. It's baked in. In fact, when faced with resistance anytime you're transforming some area of your life, that's the first place to check. Check to determine if you have a focus for or against.

Do you have competing intentions, beliefs, or values between your conscious and unconscious mind?

Has your goal genuinely been about what you want, or is it more about getting away from something you don't want?

It may be helpful to have a working definition of an obstacle. My definition of an obstacle is "a perceived limitation to achieving a desired outcome." What do you think? Do you have a different meaning?

Your perceptions and interpretations determine what you identify as an obstacle and how you respond to them. As discussed earlier, each person has their own way of responding to obstacles.

In my work with literally thousands of clients over the years I've noticed that the top four obstacles for most people when it comes to achieving a worthwhile goal are lack of clarity, unharnessed motivation, fear of failure, and fear of success.

Use Occam's Razor[32]

If you're not sure what's holding you back or what's in your way, use Occam's Razor. It's a practical principle used in science for over seven hundred years that is attributed to William of Ockham.

Paraphrased, Occam's Razor says that if there are two or more theories to account for a phenomenon, the simplest theory is the most likely to be true, because nature only operates in the simplest way.

Since the first step in solving a problem is to identify and define the problem accurately, it would be wise to use as simple a process as possible. Accuracy is important. I've heard so many people tell stories of enormous, valiant efforts to overcome their difficulties with no success. After listening to them for a little while it becomes apparent that they've been trying to solve the wrong problem.

How many millions of people are spending billions of dollars every year trying on pharmaceuticals trying to make their depression and anxiety go away? Not only does it not work, but they also continue to increase their dose and add recreational drugs. The problem is not people's anxiety and depression; those are merely symptoms. The problem is the negative focus of their thinking, and that can be easily and quickly corrected.

It's a known fact how the human mind works, how the quantum field works, and how the law of faith works. Simply, the clearer you are about what you want, the more likely you are to have it.

Being clear about who you are, what you want, and where you're going is essential to achieving better results. It also seems to be one of the most challenging steps. Every coach I've ever worked with has focused me on that step repeatedly, more than any other. The clearer I am, the better the results I achieve in life, relationships, and business.

Interview yourself. Honestly, are you clearer about what you don't want or what you do want? Do you have a precise vision of where you want to be, how you want to feel, how you want your relationship to be?

Motivation is a function of priorities. When what you say you want is too low down on your priority list, it will lead to you being distracted and easily put off course. Make a list of excuses that you commonly use to avoid doing something. Do you notice a pattern?

If your house were on fire and all it would take is a garden hose to save it, would you be so distracted by your common excuses? Probably not, if saving your house was a high enough priority. It's a miracle what you can accomplish when motivated enough.

I recall reading a story many years ago of a middle-aged woman who heard her husband scream in pain when the car he was working underneath fell on him. The story was that she ran into the garage, grabbed the running board of the vehicle and flipped it on its side, saving her husband. After he was treated and released, she was asked by investigators to see if she could lift the car again. She couldn't even budge it.

Once the crisis was over, her motivation to flip cars was pretty low. When the urgency of the moment sufficiently motivated her, even a full-sized vehicle was no obstacle. When what you want is a high enough priority no obstacle will stand in your way. Potentially superhuman ability is available to help you push through your obstacles.

A common obstacle is fear of failure, but, what does it actually mean? It seems to imply that failure is inevitable and is to be avoided at all cost. I like to remind myself and my clients what they went through when they learned how to walk, talk, and write their name. They failed repeatedly. Failure is a natural part of a learning curve.

Unfortunately, just reminding them of that wasn't enough to inspire most of them forward. The concept of failure is too loaded for far too many people, which leads to the idea that by focusing so heavily on fear of failure, what you, in fact get is exactly that – fear and failure. A coincidence? I don't believe it is.

Most people automatically do what it takes to avoid anything that elicits fear, like Miss Snake Phobia in Chapter 2. Preventing fear of failure, something that hasn't even happened yet, would also lead you to avoid trying in the first place. Even if you can push through the fear, if you're still focused on failure, guess what your unconscious mind is most likely to manifest? If you guessed 'failure,' then you are correct.

Believe it or not, many people are afraid of success, too. They've grown to kind of enjoying their cozy little hobbit hole where "they live in a gray twilight that knows not victory nor defeat."[33] Being successful means they'll be living outside the safety net. There would be more personal responsibility. It also means that once someone is successful, they'll be a more natural target for criticism and rejection.

Therefore, the desire to achieve their goal must be greater than any fear they have. Not only that, but all of their focus must be on already having arrived successfully at their destination so wholly that it's their new normal.

If you want to know how to handle criticism and rejection, re-read Chapters 1 and 2.

The next question is how you break through to the other side. What does it mean to overcome an obstacle? How do you overcome obstacles at work? How do you overcome obstacles in life?

What obstacles are you contending with now? Make a list. Accurately defining a problem is the first step in solving any problem. Write out a list of as many as you can think of. Do you notice any patterns emerging?

There are two primary outcome potentials with any obstacle. First, the obstacle may keep you from getting, doing, or being who you want, and second, the barrier can be traversed, and you arrive at your destination quite successfully.

Zig Ziglar, American author, salesman and motivational speaker, famously said that "every sale has five basic obstacles: no need, no money, no hurry, no desire, no trust."

It's like a bumper sticker I saw once that said "There are two kinds of people. Those who divide people into two kinds of people and those who don't."

Regardless of how many types of obstacles there are, it's all about how you respond to the barrier that matters most. More generally speaking, it seems to me that there are three basic categories of obstacles: "innies," "outies," and general stress.

"Innies" are the internal obstacles. They're probably the ones we struggle with the most. They're the limiting beliefs and negative emotions.

Examples of limiting beliefs are things like "this will never work," "only rotten people make money," "if I gain something good, then something bad will happen to wipe it out," "I might fail," "I'm unworthy," and so on.

Negative emotions such as fear, dread, depression, overwhelm, and paranoia require a developed skill of self-awareness to identify. When you apply the principle of focusing on what you're for, they're not too hard to change, either. The inner world requires you to be vigilant to make sure you don't slip too far into the dark side.

"Outies" are external obstacles. Some examples of "outies" are other people attempting to discourage you or lack of support, not enough time, not enough money, the weather, boulders in the road.

As Zig Ziglar pointed out, your customer may potentially have no need, no money, no hurry, no desire, or no trust. I'm given to understand that Mr. Ziglar was never held back by that. For example, a customer may have no hurry, because you haven't pointed out to them a reason to hurry. The average customer lacks focus; as a result, the need to push may never occur to them without some help. Overcoming any outward obstacle is possible: Set your intention on what you're for, engage the creative aspect designed into you by God, and move forward.

BULLDOZE THE BARRICADES: MAKING EASY WORK OF OBSTACLES

General stress is all about the effect that accumulation of stress can have over time. When overly stressed your mind has a harder time focusing, you tend to forget things, and it becomes difficult to sleep. As stress increases even more, it can result in illnesses and even death.

Look back at the Stress/Performance Curve chart in the discussion of The Zone in Chapter 6. If you're on the dark side, your symptoms can be formidable obstacles. Reducing stress is really not that hard. When you apply the proper skills and mindset, changes happen pretty quickly.

It also requires some vigilance to track where you are on the curve every day. Knowing which category of stress or obstacle you're dealing with increases your power to change the game entirely. Start by classifying the type of obstacle you've encountered. Then, narrow it down as accurately as you can from there.

"How you do anything is how you do everything."

Unknown

Probably the most crucial element in handling any obstacle is your response to the obstruction.

Do you tend to avoid? Some individuals pretend like the obstacle's not there. Maybe when they wake up from a long nap, it won't be there. Perhaps it'll go away on its own, or it's a figment of an overly active imagination. Are you a bull in a china shop? Some people choose to go in swinging or have both guns blazing away at an obstacle. There are two problems with this. Either they're pounding away at the wrong piece of china or what they resist, persists.

Both avoiders and blazers discover what some have called The Problem Solution. The Problem-Solution means that the very solution they've come up with to solve a problem has only served to create a whole new set of problems. The reality is that the problem is resistance. Both people and animals tend to resist change, even if it's change from an adverse circumstance to a better circumstance. It seems to be innate.

Obstacles represent resistance to achieving your goals. How you respond to the opposition determines the outcome. Think about your own typical manner of responding to an obstacle. Small ones might not be too big of a deal but consider what happens when you encounter the big ones. Do you become anxious, angry, hopeless, overwhelmed? Are you an avoider or a blazer?

What you focus on, increases. What you resist, persists.

> "Obstacles are necessary for success because in selling, as in all careers of importance, victory comes only after many struggles and countless defeats."
>
> Og Mandino, American author

Four Keys to Your Breakthrough

What are the keys to breaking through any obstacle? Here are four of the big ones:

1. Be clear about defining what obstacle you're facing. "Obstacles are those frightful things you see when you take your eyes off your goal." (Henry Ford)

2. Choose an effective strategy based on the type of obstacle. If it's an inward problem, identify the limiting belief and replace it with an overcoming belief. If it's an emotion, identify the negative emotion and replace it with a preferable emotion. If it's an external obstacle, it's important to specify what it is. Is it a boulder? Other people? Lack of time?

3. Clarify what you could achieve if this obstacle weren't holding you back. What would you experience on the other side? Be very, very, clear.

4. Maintain your new focus until you arrive on the other side at your destination.

Alternative Strategies

If the steps above aren't too helpful, consider one of the following alternative strategies.

First, increase clarity about your goal. Be able to feel it and taste it. Raise your sense of priority about achieving it to the highest level in your mind. If it was the most critical thing in the world for you to achieve, what would you do differently? Whatever you focus on gets bigger. If you're obsessed with the obstacle to the exclusion of the goal, you'll get more resistance to overcoming the obstacle.

In other words, you'll get more obstacle and less overcoming. When you focus explicitly on the goal, your highly creative unconscious mind will begin formulating solutions that would blow away your conscious mind.

On a personal note, I've played around with merely visualizing the obstacle turning to dust. Then I zero in on as clear an image of my goal as I can muster. The majority of the time, the obstruction vanishes in the real world. What I take from that is it was my internal resistance that created the obstacle in the first place. It wasn't the economy, other people, or lack of resources. It was me. When I shifted into goal achieving, obstacle dissolving mode, I moved forward exponentially, and the obstacle dissolved.

Next, identify the smallest step possible that you can take today to achieve your goal, regardless of the obstacle. Ask yourself what is the smallest step you can take before 7PM today that will move you forward to your goal, regardless of any obstacle. Whatever the answer is, do it.

Believe it or not, this strategy is surprisingly effective!

I once had a coaching client from Canada who had felt stuck for five years in her ability to get back to being a painter. She had been to a therapist for a couple of years and still was stuck. She described her block as a very high cement wall, many feet thick and extending forever in both directions. It went deep into the ground and was impenetrable.

Instead of focusing on the wall, I asked her, "What's the smallest step you could take to get to the other side of the wall?" Without hesitation, she said that it would be to lay out her painting tarp. So, that became her assignment. She agreed to lay out her tarp before the next visit a week later.

On our next call, she said she'd laid out the tarp and immediately began painting. She'd been painting for five days when she hadn't even been in that room for the five years prior!

One, small, step and BOOM! The obstacle dissolved.

Third, ask yourself the intention question. Although you've already learned about the intention question in Chapter 5, I have another example for you that is more about overcoming an obstacle of being stuck. As you recall, the intention question is one of the best types in the universe that you can ask to overcome almost any obstacle or solve practically any problem.

In a significantly less mature era of my life, I experienced an incident while driving my pickup truck north of town in early April. There'd been a lot of snow that year, and it was beginning to melt. I thought it would be fun to drive off the road and explore a bit down a canal bank in the late evening. About a quarter of a mile off the main roadway I began sinking into the mud. I climbed out of the truck and used every trick I could think of to get out. I got the jack out, lifted it up and put chains on it. I put boards under the tires. It didn't budge.

The thought came to me to ask the intention question. "What's the best way to get this truck out of the mud?" Within seconds I realized that the mud would freeze in a few hours and I could drive out with no problem.

I hitched a ride back to the dorm, cleaned up, and asked someone to take me back out there at 4:30 the next morning. By 5AM the mud had frozen, and I was able to drive the vehicle out immediately with no problem.

I learned a lot of lessons from that experience, but most importantly, it's an excellent example of how counterintuitive some of the best strategies are for overcoming obstacles.

Finally, when encountering resistance from others learn how to use the power of acknowledgment. One of the top needs of most people is to be accurately understood and acknowledged to their satisfaction by others. It's truly rare for us to have someone correctly acknowledge us to our satisfaction, which is why so many people go to counselors. They're desperately trying to find someone to listen to and understand them. It's a shame that even very few counselors have any idea how to do that.

To correctly acknowledge someone is to say back to them what you've heard them say as accurately as possible without adding any spin or your own opinions, only what they genuinely desire for you to understand.

It doesn't have to be hard. Keep it simple and extremely accurate.

For example, there have been a couple of incidents in which I had a linebacker-sized oil field worker in my office become violently angry with me because I dared to suggest they not abuse their wife anymore.

Fists balled up, they stood up as if to come over and hit me, but when I carefully and calmly summarized what I'd heard them say, at least twice the guys sat back down and began crying like babies.

That's what neutralized resistance looks like.

So many people will escalate their volume and intensity when trying to get you to understand something, especially if you don't acknowledge them. Watch what happens when you carefully and accurately summarize their point. All of the intensity seems to disappear into the woodwork or dribble down the drain.

All obstacles have a way to the other side. The key is in the quality of your focus and mindset.

Boundaries

"Givers need to set limits because takers rarely do."

Rachel Wolchin, American writer

Having difficulty with the demands and expectations of others is another type of obstacle that many don't think of as an obstacle. Having poor limits can easily derail you from accomplishing goals and drain vital energy from your life. Notice what happens if you extend your hand to someone as if to shake their hand. Most people will automatically take your hand, even if they don't want to. In the same way, you'd probably take their hand and feel awkward if you didn't. It's an example of how boundaries can be manipulated by people who intuitively utilize that awkwardness to get what they want.

Think about what happens when a manipulative salesperson talks you into buying something you don't want. You've probably felt guilty enough for saying no that you went ahead and spent money needlessly. There's primarily one problem that creates poor boundaries. That problem is lack of clarity about what you want. The solution is boundaries. The key to healthy boundaries is becoming clear about what you want, who you are, where you end, and where the other person begins.

Most of the quotes I've seen on social media suggest that it's the other person's fault for not respecting our boundaries. For example, "No. Is a complete sentence." (Anne Lamott). At face value, there's nothing wrong with that quote. It seems practical and accurate.

On the other hand, such a quote seems to imply that the boundary violator needs to get with the program and respect other people saying "No." It further suggests that the other person is responsible for knowing and maintaining your boundaries. In reality, each person is responsible for their boundaries. The hardest part seems to be getting over feeling guilty about how the other person might feel.

It's common for many to use anger and threats to enforce a boundary. Unfortunately, it doesn't work very well. Anger conveys anything but confidence. It communicates that you're out of control. The potential boundary violator knows that you can't sustain being angry indefinitely, so they have only to wait a few minutes to try again. Eventually, most people will give in.

To have clear, firm boundaries, first be clear about exactly what you want. Do you want to say, no and mean it? Do you want to say yes and mean it? Or, is there something else? Secondly, use the white tiger strategy to transform feelings of guilt into calmness, or quiet confidence. Use mental rehearsal to practice over and over until you become an expert.

Practice your boundaries every chance you get. Review your progress, troubleshoot, and practice some more. When you're crystal clear about what you want and who you are, others will naturally sense your boundaries and behave accordingly. Eventually, you'll only need a glance to convey a solid, "No."

CHAPTER EIGHT
THE TRUTH ABOUT POWER: A LITTLE BIT GOES A LONG WAY

The Problem of Power

> "If you realized how powerful your thoughts are, you would never think a negative thought."
>
> Peace Pilgrim, American non-denominational spiritual teacher, mystic pacifist, and vegetarian and peace activist

This book is all about the incredible power you have to master a life worth living from the inside out. You have tremendous potential. Everyone does. It's vitally important to learn about your power and how to properly use it, otherwise, you'll merely circle a huge drain in your life and go precisely nowhere.

For the majority of those I've met, power is a problem in one way or another. They either think they have no control or know they're powerful and try to avoid it. It's not so much that they believe they're powerless or vulnerable. The problem is that to them, power means something very adverse.

Consider the example of a child abused by a bully. The innocent child would naturally interpret the bully as being powerful. The victim would interpret themselves as powerless by comparison. The dominant person is interpreted as dangerous and potent. The victim seems innocent and weak.

Later on, the victim would associate having power with the bully. They could develop a belief that only bullies are powerful, or that if they have power, they must be a bully, as well. Perhaps they believe that power is evil.

It's for similar reasons that some people who are victimized by bullies at a young age will become bullies. They desperately want to be powerful. Others find comfort in giving up their power. They'd rather be vulnerable than to be a bully to avoid being evil. It depends on which is more important to them at the time.

Power is power. It's only either good or bad depending on its use. For example, a surgical scalpel can be used by a skilled physician to heal humans or animals. The same blade can be used by a psychopath to kill. In reality, the scalpel is just a scalpel. It's a razor-sharp instrument.

> "The greatest weapon against stress is our ability to choose one thought over another."
>
> William James, American philosopher and psychologist

Having the power to choose one thought over another seems to many like it's way too simple to be taken seriously as a form of power. The truth is that having the power to choose your thoughts is formidable. That power can transform one emotion into another. It can convert a life that's not working to a better life. A marriage, a community, and even an entire world can shift from bad to good and from good to great depending on which thoughts you choose.

Even though it's profoundly simple, it's still a form of power. Because of that, a large percentage of people avoid using it. They choose to stay right where they're at rather than to use their power and risk seeming evil. If power is a problem for you, it's time to take a look at your belief about power. Once you're willing to transform your false beliefs, you'll be free to choose the new thought that will bring you closer to the life you love.

Excel at being a benevolent, powerful person.

The Power of Follow Through

> "There is no breakthrough without follow through."
>
> Unknown

Have you ever played tennis, baseball, golf, or practiced karate? They all have something in common. When you learn how to perform these sports, your instructor will in some way teach you the importance of follow through.

When I was in my mid-teens, I was in a full contact karate class. I mentioned in the section about grounding and centering that I'd learned how to ground and center from that karate instructor. He also taught me about the power of follow through.

Breaking a board using a typical martial arts punch is less painful than it might seem. It isn't so easy if you focus on the board. If you focus on the board or the brick, you'll unconsciously tend to stop just before the board. When that happens, the board won't break, and your hand easily could break. It's painful, trust me. Any experienced instructor will teach you to imagine your hand following a line from yourself, through the board, off to the horizon. It takes some practice to follow that path instead of focusing on the board.

The first time I followed through correctly, the board broke with what seemed like no effort at all. My hand hardly felt it.

The same thing happened when a friend of mine took me to the driving range to help me with my swing. He'd grown up on a golf course. He watched my swing a few times and noticed I was moving my hips just before hitting the ball, and I seemed to stop just before the club made contact with the ball.

He told me to keep my hips still and to follow through with the club. Where had I heard that before? So, that's what I did in my next swing. My hips remained still, and I followed through. With a fraction of the energy I'd ever used in a swing before, the ball sailed what seemed to be over 200 yards! It was astonishing.

As a freshman in my earliest college days, I took a tennis class. I'd played tennis quite a bit before that, mainly hacking at the ball and frequently wanting to throw my racket as far as I could and never see another one again. During one of our classes, the instructor observed my serve. He then demonstrated the exact proper form for a good serve. I practiced the form until I had it down, then tried a serve. Even though I had perfect form, I still tended to hesitate at the point of contacting the ball. There was no telling where the ball would wind up, but in the court on the other side of the net was rarely it.

You guessed it. The instructor showed me how to follow through. It took some practice to over-ride my tendency to stop midway, but after some successful practice, I lobbed a ball, used perfect form and followed through. With a fraction of the power I'd ever used with a tennis racket, I smacked that ball, and it rocketed just over the net flawlessly into the right spot on the other side.

I didn't play much baseball, but I know it's the same idea. Learn the proper form for swinging and follow through! The ball goes much farther with a fraction of the energy.

Follow through applies to all areas of life. Especially to any area of life in which you'd like to accomplish a particular outcome. Listen to anyone's story of how they've failed to achieve some goal in life, including your own story. In every case, you'll notice it all stopped at the point where they were focused, usually the obstacle. Any time you stop short, it means that you've not learned the skill of follow through.

Get clear about your target goal. Imagine a pathway from your heart straight through any obstacles, straight through your goal, and off into outer space. Imagine flowing along that pathway all the way into space with complete abandon. Rehearse it over and over until you realize one day that you've achieved your goal.

A practical example happened in 2010 when I wrote my first eBook. I'd had the idea for years but repeatedly fell short in the follow-through department. While in a coaching program I was professionally "nagged" until I completed the book, listed it online, and sold several copies.

When I paused to look back on the process the first thought in my mind was, "That wasn't that hard. What was I so worried about?" The truth was that the hardest part was flowing through all of the neurotically perceived obstacles on the way. None of them were real.

When you follow through, you'll have the breakthrough in creating a life worth living.

Types of Power

Now and then I reflect on the main obstacles that various clients, loved ones, and I encounter. Sometimes it's a problem with being indecisive, lacking awareness or focus, or blocking beliefs. The list keeps growing. As I ponder each characteristic, it's occurred to me that each is a form of power in its own right.

Here's a list of a few obstacles and types of power. By no means do I think this is the entire list and I'm sure over time I'll probably add more as they come to mind.

Some may seem like they're two different words for the same thing, such as the words "decision," and "choice;" but they're not the same thing.

Anytime you feel powerless or out of control, take a look at this list.

Types of Power

1. Power of intention;
2. Decision;
3. Choice;
4. Awareness;
5. Personal responsibility;
6. Forgiveness;
7. Love;
8. Focus;

9. Rest;
10. Confession - Proclamation;
11. Belief;
12. Imagination;
13. Expectations;
14 Priorities;
15. Giving;
16. Receiving;
17. Perspective;
18. Attitude;
19. Follow through;
20. Clarity;
21. Leverage;
22. Words;
23. Listening;
24. Faith;
25. Silence;
26. Surrender;
27. The Power of God.

Many of these have already been mentioned at one point or another in this book. I think an entire book could be written on each one. Here are a few words to consider about each.

1. The Power of Intention

> "We either live with intention or exist by default."
>
> Kristin Armstrong, professional road bicycle racer and three-time Olympic Gold medalist

Intention is the power of your aim. When you aim your eyes to the middle of the road in front of you, your vehicle will tend to drift in that direction. Your mind is like an eye. In the same way that you'll tend to drive in the direction that your eyes are looking, your life will tend to drift in the direction that your mind is thinking.

In the same way that you can change the direction that your eyes are looking, you can change the thoughts of your mind. A minimal change in your thoughts can create an enormous difference in your life. That's a lot of power.

2. The Power to Decide

> "Be decisive. Right or wrong, make a decision. The road of life is paved with flat squirrels who couldn't make a decision."
>
> (Unknown)

The word "decide" comes from the Latin language. "De" which means "of" and the other part of the word, "caedere," means "to cut." To decide literally means to cut off.

The idea is that an actual decision cuts off all alternatives but one. Let's say you're in a position in which you need to choose among three bridges to cross. Suppose you decide to cross over bridge number 2. To decide to cross bridge number 2 means that you're cutting off the choice to take bridges number 1 and 3. You're also cutting off bridge number 2 behind you as you go. There's no turning back. You're all in.

North Americans have become pretty sloppy in how they use language. They are famous for saying something like, "I decided to quit my dead-end job a year ago and find a job I love and make more money, but, I still haven't done it."

Apparently, you didn't decide. You certainly thought about it. If you'd decided to quit your job you'd already be doing your dream job or well on your way.

How can you tell what a person has decided to do? By results. You can decide to do something, you can decide not to do something; or, you can decide not to decide. If you decide not to decide, you've decided not to do it.

I've worked with over a thousand people whose lives were ruined when they decided at some point in their life to believe that they're unworthy of having a life worth living. Once they made the decision, the unconscious mind made sure they remained consistent with that decision. I've also met hundreds of people who can point to a moment in their life when they decided to thrive and create a prosperous life. And they did.

That's a lot of power.

3. The Power of Choice

    "Be miserable. Or motivate yourself. Whatever has to be done, it's always your choice."

    Wayne Dyer

In our ordinary way of speaking, we tend to use language such as, "I don't have any choices," or, "I have too many choices, I don't know what to do." They're not choices. They're alternatives. To choose is to pick one of the other options.

Everyone has more than one alternative in life. There is more than one emotion available. There is more than one belief. Choosing one and developing it is a fantastic power. It's much like the power of deciding.

4. The Power of Awareness

> "Without self-awareness, we are as babies in the cradles."
>
> Virginia Woolf, English modernist
> 20th-century writer

I estimate that ninety-five percent of the population is unaware of how they're feeling at any one time. They'd swear they know exactly how they are doing, but even an untrained observer can tell what's going on in them.

Awareness is all about taking an inventory of what's happening for you, both inside and out. How are you feeling? What are you thinking? What are your strengths? What patterns in your life serve you? Which work against you? Emotions usually show up as physical symptoms. For example, anxiety often manifests as tension in the chest, stomach, shoulders, or throat.

Knowing what's going on can be a powerful tool you can use to get an edge on making a course correction as quickly as possible before a negative becomes too well established.

5. Personal Responsibility

> "You must take personal responsibility. You cannot change the circumstances, the seasons, or the wind, but you can change yourself."
>
> Jim Rohn, American entrepreneur,
> author and motivational speaker

Since what is going on and where you're going are a by-product of what's happening from the innermost you outwardly, blaming others is irrelevant. Taking personal responsibility for your own thoughts, feelings, and actions is where actual effectiveness begins. No one else can do it for you.

6. Forgiveness

> "If we really want to love we must learn how to forgive."
>
> Mother Theresa, Saint Theresa of Calcutta, Roman Catholic nun and missionary

Forgiveness is a commonly misunderstood concept. Some believe that to forgive is a form of weakness. Unforgiveness is a like a ball and chain that only seems to grow larger and more cumbersome with the passage of time. Forgiveness is freeing for all who practice it entirely.

Some people are hesitant to forgive because of a belief that forgiveness condones what the offender did. In no way is forgiveness the same as condoning any offender or offense. Some people's forgiveness has conditions attached, for example they say that they could forgive if they knew the offender didn't mean it.

There are false teachings about forgiveness such as to forgive is to forget, or that if you forgive someone that you have to trust them. Both are completely false.

The Bible is where we truly learn about forgiveness. The Bible doesn't teach to forgive and forget. It doesn't show that to forgive someone is to trust them. Forgiveness and trust are two different concepts. In fact, Jeremiah 17:5 says, "Thus says the LORD: "Cursed is the man who trusts in man and makes flesh his strength...."

We are commanded to trust only God. We're also commanded to forgive everyone, including our enemies.

Trust and forgiveness are not the same things. It's possible to forgive and love your enemies and yet not trust them any farther than you can throw a bus.

Biblically, forgiveness is an accounting term. When someone was owed a debt and wanted the debt canceled, the lender drew a line through it. They canceled the debt. The saying was that they "remembered it against them no more." Canceling the debt is profoundly freeing and healing. God expects it as a minimum condition for being His child.

7. Love

> "I'm fully convinced that the greatest thing you can do for someone; the most Jesus-like, most God-honoring thing, is to err on the side of loving them."
>
> John Pavlovitz, American Christian pastor and author

Love is a form of power. It's a force. God is Love. God is the author of all life. Loving and being loved creates and sustains life in humans, animals, and even plants. In the last two hundred years, many have come to regard love as nothing more than a feeling. Although feeling might be involved, love is also a verb. Children who receive too little love can develop what is called "failure to thrive."

God commands us to love our enemies. It would be enormously difficult to do that if you depended on a feeling. Love must be something more significant and different than a feeling. Remember that feelings follow facts, which is another way of saying that feelings are the result of your belief about an event. When your beliefs change, your emotions change even if your belief is entirely false.

In today's world, many divorces happen after one or both spouses justify leaving each other because they've fallen out of love. People in second and third world countries think that's hilarious. Long-term studies have shown that couples who are in arranged marriages tend to fall in love with one another in about two years after being married. Arranged marriages typically have a foundation based on a sense of duty.

The idea of being in love as a prerequisite for marriage or being out of love as a reason for divorce is absurd to people in cultures where arranged marriages are the norm. Such unions also tend to last a lifetime, and divorce is much less frequent.

Love leads to life. When a child, animal, or plant is loved they thrive. When they're either not loved or are actively hated, they wither and die. That seems to imply some correlation. Love has been defined as working in the best interest of another. That's an excellent example of how love is a verb.

On the other hand, what would it mean if you have a heart filled with love for someone? That implies that there is at least positive emotion for another person. Let's take this to another level. The evidence seems to support the idea that love is a force. How does that work? Love is an emotion on some level. It's also working in the best interest of another, regardless of your sentiment. At the same time, love affects you and others in a positive, life-giving way.

That reminds me of how quantum faith works. When you have faith the size of a mustard seed and do not doubt in your heart creation must obey you. The information passes into the Quantum Field, and things happen at a distance. In the same way, it seems that love creates effects in the Quantum Field and can affect others at a distance. Love always works in an affirmative, healing, healthful direction. It's a force to be reckoned with. How being loving positively affects you and others is naturally healthful. No wonder God commands us to forgive and love everyone, including our enemies.

8. Focus

> "Your focus influences your emotions. Your emotions influence your behavior. Your behavior determines your results. Your results determine your outcomes. Your outcomes determine your destiny. You can control your destiny by controlling your focus."
>
> (Unknown)

Focus refers to not only where you're looking but how clearly you see. You'll tend to drift in the direction that your eyes and mind are looking. Clarity of focus makes an enormous difference in your destiny. The clearer your goal, the more likely you are to achieve it.

9. Rest

> "In returning and rest you shall be saved;
> in quietness and in trust shall be your strength."
>
> Isaiah 30:15

Rest helps to calm your arousal state. Being calm and focused is a formidable combination. Anxiety constricts awareness into a form of tunnel vision. The more anxious and stressed you are, the more you're looking at life through a straw. The closer you are to an at-rest state, the more comfortably aware you are of yourself and everything around you. You can be in an at-rest state while walking, running, driving, or even working. Whoever thought we'd have to practice to rest?

Rest is a state of mind and soul. The ultimate rest is to have rest for your soul. To have rest for your soul is to practice complete trust in God. It's profoundly moving to see a small baby sleeping soundly in complete trust of the one taking care of them. That's what it can be like when we fully trust God.

The most talented warriors, martial artists, and athletes describe being in a calm, rested state before and as they perform at what appears to be a superhuman level. They've come to know who they are and what they can do. No time is spent on anxiety, only performing how they've trained. God strictly enforced the Jewish people to practice a day of rest called the Sabbath Day. Several religious groups practice a variation of the Sabbath today.

The Harvard Business Review published a great article in October 2009 entitled *Making Time Off Predictable—and Required*, by Leslie A. Perlow and Jessica L. Porter. The authors researched for four years in several offices of the Boston Consulting Group, in which they challenged consultants and other professionals to maintain their high standards while taking planned, uninterrupted time off.

> "Indeed, we found that when the assumption that everyone needs to be always available was collectively challenged, not only could individuals take time off, but their work actually benefited. Our experiments with time off resulted in more open dialogue among team members, which is valuable in itself. But the improved communication also

sparked new processes that enhanced the teams' ability to work most efficiently and effectively.

Taking even one, uninterrupted day off in our high demand world is intensely counter-intuitive, isn't it? You'd think it would be comfortable and enjoyable. When I've practiced taking a full, uninterrupted day, I can feel all kinds of nerves twitching and haunting dialogue from the back of my head telling me about all the things I should be doing instead and how much time I'm wasting. I have to squash those pesky thoughts. Rest helps to restore you and me psychologically, emotionally, and physically."

Rest for your soul happens best when you surrender yourself by faith to God. That's a whole subject for a different book in itself.

10. Confession-Proclamation

> "Be impeccable with your word. Speak with integrity. Say only what you mean. Avoid using the word to speak against yourself or to gossip about others. Use the power of your word in the direction of truth and love."
>
> Don Miguel Ruiz, Mexican autor of Toltec spiritualist and neoshamanistic texts

Saying something out loud seems to increase dramatically the manifestation of what is said. Thinking of something is one thing but speaking it aloud seems to create a contract with the universe making what you utter a reality.

Notice what Romans 10:10 says. "For with the heart one believes and is, and with the mouth confesses and is saved." (ESV) Confessing belief out loud can complete the salvation process. What you say can bless, curse, and create. What you have been saying has played a crucial role in your quality of life.

11. Belief

> "Whether you think you can, or think you can't, you're right."
>
> Henry Ford, American captain of industry and business magnate, founder of the Ford Motor Company

Belief has already been discussed a good bit in this book. Jesus spoke a great deal about belief. Therefore, it's essential to take some time to use the power of awareness to discover what you believe. Use what you're learning to transform them into true, positive beliefs. In so doing, you'll reprogram your life from the inside out.

12. Imagination – the Lens of the Mind

> "You can't depend on your eyes when your imagination is out of focus."
>
> Mark Twain, American writer, humorist, entrepreneur, publisher, and lecturer

The eyes are the windows to the soul. In the same way, your mind is the window to your state. Your mind works like a lens, much like the lens of your eyes. What you focus on affects your entire life. In particular, it influences your beliefs, emotions, behavior, and spirituality. It changes how you see the world, yourself, other people, God, and the decisions you make. The choices you make affect how you respond to each situation and eventually where you wind up down the road.

Your mind has a lens, just like your eyes do. That lens is responsible for seeing the world around you, whether in focus or out of focus. It's responsible for the spin that guides your decisions and so on. It's affected by your beliefs, interpretations, and expectations. If your lens is dirty, it can distort what you see and how you interpret what you see. The lens of your mind is affected by various experiences and influences in your life, such as the opinions of your parents, teachers, close friends, your accurate and inaccurate interpretations of the world, and so on.

Pink elephants are notorious for leading some great people into some seriously funky places in the jungle. All because of dirty lenses.

After a couple of centuries of research, we know that your perceptions and interpretations influence your beliefs. Your beliefs precipitate your emotional responses for either the good or the bad. Your actions are a result of your beliefs and emotions. The three together create your life the way it is now. We've all at one time or another said that another person "made" use angry or that something "terrified" us. The implication is that the other person is responsible for our anger or that the snake terrified them. Wow! That means that other people and snakes have a fantastic amount of power. They can force us to feel all kinds of negative things. We should simply give up.

But, wait! What about Larry and Bob? They're both in their early thirties and attending the local university. It's almost lunchtime, so they decide to walk to a nearby fast food joint. As they approach the intersection, there's an unfortunate accident. Although there are no deaths, there are some injuries. Before they get to the intersection, EMTs are already on the scene.

Just before they cross at the crosswalk, Larry runs over to a bush and throws up. Bob is confused. He asks Larry what's going on. Larry replies that the accident made him sick. Bob's response? He wants Larry to hurry up because he's hungry!

According to Larry, that accident was so powerful that it MADE him sick, but Bob didn't get sick. He's even more hungry now. The men had two completely different states in reaction to the same event. Larry has bought into the belief that his circumstances are responsible for his feelings. The truth is that Larry had never seen anything like that before and didn't have a reference point for it. He engaged the belief that he couldn't handle it and his body responded accordingly.

Bob was an EMT for ten years. He used to eat his lunch with his buddies cleaning up accident sites on the highway. Seeing an accident site brings back some fond memories. It "makes" him hungry. Bob has a different filter or lens. When you're interpreting the world with a dirty lens, your interpretation of the world is distorted. It could make a whole lot of things look just like pink elephants.

Those of us who wear glasses for any reason can relate to that. It's astonishing how quickly they can get dirty, within minutes after cleaning. Just blinking a bunch or squinting doesn't help much. If your filter is dirty or distorted then your perceptions, interpretations, and beliefs will be affected. You'll be vulnerable to all kinds of strange emotional and behavioral reactions. The way in which you interpret any given situation will determine what you believe about it and how you'll respond.

The accident Larry and Bob witnessed is what is referred to as an "activating event." It has no power. It's benign. It's just an event. Your response to the event is based on the filter. The filter consists of your beliefs, interpretations, and expectations. Those factors have been shaped since our early childhood. You've been accumulating these smudges on your lens without ever questioning them. The good news is that the filter can be cleaned. Your imagination can be calibrated to the truth and disciplined to correct for all kinds of distortions.

No one can force you to feel anything. It's simply not possible. No snake can make you feel scared. No one can make you mad or hurt your feelings. Any scared feeling involving a snake that you might experience is just a matter of the beliefs, interpretations, and expectations happening in your filter. Any hurt feelings about someone else is a result of the same thing.

If you can be free of hurt, anxiety, and anger, a crucial question is left in that emptiness. How would you rather feel?

> "You can't control how other people receive your energy. Anything you do or say gets filtered through the lens of whatever they are going through at the moment, which is not about you. Just keep doing your thing with as much integrity and love as possible."
>
> Nanea Hoffman, writer and founder of Sweatpants & Coffee, a popular blog

The Spirit Effect

Did you ever struggle with having a robust and intimate relationship with God? Everyone I've ever known who has sought God sincerely has a story of how much they've fought at some point in their relationship with God. You might have started out on fire for God, passionate about who He is for you and your rich future with the God of the universe. Everything may start out just fine for the first few months or years. Then, you run into hardships, difficult people, abusive church goers, financial problems, and so on.

Those difficulties can lead to some negative assumptions about who you are, whether God has forsaken you, whether or not you're being punished, whether The Bible is even real. For most of us, the solution is simple. We need a lens change.

We are meant to look at the whole truth of God and then look at what we are seeing and believing, and does it really line up with Scripture? If it doesn't, we have to change that lens. I don't care who gave you that lens. I don't care if you got it in Bible cemetery, seminary... Freudian slip there (possibly).

> "If the Word of God is different than your lens, there is only one possibility for change! You know, our lenses, our assumptions, our way of seeing the world, they shape how we interpret The Bible. They shape how we relate to God and people and the world When you see your lens, you can begin to evaluate them consciously. Really, the witness of the Spirit is designed to empower you to see something different if something different needs to be seen. Does your lens need to be cleaned?"
>
> Graham Cooke, from *The Portland Sessions, School of Prophecy*

When we encounter various trials, difficult people, uncertain circumstances, and a plethora of other problems, our old lens distortions come up quickly.

As a young person, I owned a couple of telescopes and microscopes that had more than one lens for more than one purpose. Occasionally, a lens had to be changed to get a more accurate view of my target. In the same way, we all need a lens change when it comes to our walk with God. It may seem overly simple to just change a lens, but it can be done.

From personal experience, I can testify to how quickly my state and circumstances change for the better when I replace God's lens with my old one. A lens change may be the missing ingredient to taking your spiritual life to a ten.

13. Expectations

> "High expectations are the key to everything."
>
> Sam Walton, American businessman and entrepreneur best known for founding the retailers Walmart and Sam's Club

Expectations are a form of intention. In a loose sense, they're also a kind of prophecy. What you expect is a type of power. People who engage in what psychologists call, "catastrophic thinking," believe that if they expect the worst to happen, then whatever actually winds up happening won't be as bad. If the worst does wind up happening they can justify their predictions. Either way, they're right. Their belief is that they prophesied the outcome and it happened simply because it was prophesied by their expectation.

The irony is that their expectation is what brings about the negative outcome in first place. Even if something really good happens instead, they don't know what to do with it and tend to reject it as an anomaly.

Catastrophic thinking almost routinely leads to depression. It can also lead to becoming a "negaholic," that is, someone addicted to negative thinking. It's depressing to even talk about it. After working many years with many people, I've come to notice that, in general, other people will tend to live up to your expectations. If you genuinely expect others to love you, they will. If you expect them to hate you and reject you, they will.

Remember Sheila's story from Chapter 4?

Up until my mid-twenties, I could never figure out why so many people seemed to dislike me. A wise psychologist I met helped me to understand that I was expecting people to dislike me. They picked up that message in the sub-space field and responded accordingly. With practice, I learned to expect people to love me, and guess what? The majority complied with that expectation, as well.

If you expect your children to listen to you and comply with your requests, they will. That is if you are genuine in what you expect. When your expectation is extremely clear, you'll unconsciously set into motion forces and factors that will ensure compliance. Children who are non-compliant or even oppositional are that way many times because the expectation of the parent is either wishy-washy, or the parent expects the child to be non-compliant. A good analogy is what you learn when you take a dog obedience training class. The one who needs to be trained is the dog owner. Dogs are eager to comply. They just need to clearly understand what you expect.

When you expect the best of yourself, you'll tend to live up to your expectation of you.

14. Priorities

> "If it is important to you, you will find a way. If not, you'll find an excuse."
>
> Ryan Blair, American entrepreneur and author, co-founder and CEO of ViSalus Sciences

For years I've referred to what I call the principle of priorities." It's a powerful concept. Priorities are what you place first, second, and third in your life. That which is most important to you is that which will automatically come first in your life. Your mind will then naturally re-arrange everything else to support your primary priority. It's possible that you won't even consciously know what is most important to you. Others can tell. Just ask them what they've observed about you. The more what they tell you irritates you, the more likely that it's true.

Let's say I have a little coaster in my office for people to set drinks on. On some unconscious level, I've decided to value that coaster above everything else in my life. That coaster sits there day after day virtually unnoticed. If there were a devastating fire that wipes out the whole building, the firefighters would be scratching their heads as they looked at my charred body in the parking lot clutching a coaster with a death grip. Everything else would be lost, except that coaster. The reason is that my unconscious mind would make sure it survived the ordeal. There would be no conscious thought to it.

Priorities play an essential role in your motivation. As mentioned earlier, motivation is a by-product of your priorities. If something is important enough to you, your motivation will increase to achieve your goal. Priorities also play a key role in your relationships. Countless marriages have failed because one spouse perceives that they're not important to their mate.

A common example is when a wife claims that she doesn't feel that her husband loves her. When she accuses him of that, he responds defensively because he's not aware of what she's talking about. The majority of the time, she's right. She's not the most important person to him in the world, but he hasn't made that decision with conscious intent. It's just that over time he's gradually put something else like work, football, hunting, or his friends first. He's quite unaware of the change. When he reprioritizes his wife to be most important, his brain will restructure everything else around her brilliantly.

Priorities play a key role in your financial success. Suppose you prioritize comfort so highly that you're unwilling to get up off your tush and do what it takes to make money. Unless you're a trust fund baby, you'll probably have a hard time becoming wealthy. When wealth is made a higher priority than comfort, I'd bet a stack of $100 bills three feet high that you'll eventually be quite wealthy. Priorities can be changed. It turns out that priorities are a by-product of intention and choice. That sounds familiar. A pattern is forming, if you hadn't already seen it.

15. Giving

> "Give, and it will be given to you. Good measure pressed down, shaken together, running over, will be put into your lap. For with the measure you use it will be measured back to you."
>
> Luke 6:38

Giving is counterintuitive to a negative person who possesses a mentality of scarcity. They believe that to give is to lose and that giving away any of what they have could lead to death. Thankfully, the universe in which we live is created by God. God teaches that there is abundance, but there are principles for accessing that abundance.

Proverbs 28:27 says that "Whoever gives to the poor will not want…," and Proverbs 19:17 "Whoever is generous to the poor lends to the Lord, and he will repay him for his deed."

Giving to the poor is powerful. God has deep compassion for the poor. To give to the poor is to honor and be like Christ. Jesus promises that when we give, we will also receive. If you've not been receiving, do a little inventory about how well you've been giving.

Sociologists have identified what is called, "the exchange theory of power." Basically, if I scratch your back enough, you'll scratch mine. It's how giving and receiving happen in society. When you give to others, they'll have a natural tendency to give to you.

16. Receiving

> "If you wish for light, be ready to receive the light."
>
> Rumi, 13th-century Persian Sunni Muslim poet, jurist, Islamic scholar, theologian, and Sufi mystic

The apostle Paul said in Acts 20:35 that Jesus said, "It's more blessed to give than to receive."

I find it ironic that I've met hundreds of people, including myself, that have become quite good at giving, and yet had a difficult time receiving. It winds up being like driving down the road with at least one flat tire.

The problem wasn't that I didn't give. I gave and gave. The problem was that I wasn't receiving. All I had to do was imagine someone handing me an envelope with $5,000 in it and giving it to me with no strings attached. I noticed that I would have a hard time receiving it. I could discuss until I turn blue in the face what the reasons might be that I'd had a hard time receiving, but the bottom line is that I resisted receiving and needed to open myself up to it. The why is irrelevant. If I only give but don't receive the pipeline is plugged on one end, and the flow is restricted. Pretty soon, I won't have enough to give.

How easy is it for you to receive a compliment? Most people offer compliments sincerely. Of course, it may depend on how you'd like to be acknowledged. A beautiful woman may find it nauseating for others to continually tell her how beautiful she is. She may crave to be complimented for how good of a job she did or how intelligent she is instead, but even then, if she has a hard time receiving, it may bounce right off.

To lovingly and genuinely receive opens up the pipeline to an unrestricted flow of giving and receiving. Flow is good.

17. Perspective

> "The moment you change your perception is the moment you rewrite the chemistry in your body."
>
> Dr. Bruce Lipton, American developmental biologist best known for promoting epigenetics.[34]

Perspective is how you look at yourself, others, and life.

When you look at yourself in the mirror every day, you have a certain interpretation of what you think about yourself. What if you imagined standing in the doorway of your bedroom watching yourself look in the mirror? That's a different perspective on you. It changes your understanding of you in the context of your bedroom. What if you look at yourself through the camera of a drone 800 feet above your house looking at you looking at yourself in the mirror?

Looking at life from only one prospective can be myopic. Multiple perspectives can provide a more accurate understanding.

I once met a woman who'd had headaches due to eye problems since she was a child. When I met her, she was in her mid-forties. She told me about some surgery she'd just had on the muscles in her eyes that was believed by the surgeon to be necessary to correct the problem. After the bandages were removed from her eyes following the surgery, however, she became intensely dizzy and nauseous. Her brain had a terrible time trying to interpret what she was seeing.

It took the doctors a while to figure out that she had only seen two dimensionally all of her life up until that moment. Once the surgery was complete she could see in three dimensions, and it was severely disorienting. She had to have someone train her to handle the information.

If your perspective stinks, get a different perspective.

18. Attitude

There's a lot of truth to the often-quoted statement by Zig Ziglar that "your attitude determines your altitude."

One of the definitions of attitude found in the Merriam-Webster dictionary that applies is, " a feeling or emotion toward a fact or state. A negative attitude. An optimistic attitude."

An attitude is either a negative or positive bias toward a fact, a state, a person, or anything else. Attitude influences outcome.

When flying a fixed wing aircraft, attitude refers to whether the nose of the aircraft is up, down, or level. When the attitude of the nose is up with a normal power setting, your altitude will increase. Your altitude will decrease if the nose is toward the ground.

When your attitude is positive, all areas of your life begin to improve.

19. Follow Through

> "It was character that got us out of bed, commitment that moved us into action, and discipline that enabled us to follow through."
>
> Zig Ziglar

There's already an entire section in this chapter about follow through.

Follow through starts with imagining a pathway from you, through any obstacles, to your goal and beyond. Imagine that the obstacles are irrelevant because, in reality, they are. It just takes practice.

20. Clarity

> "Clarity attracts, confusion repels."
>
> Kary Oberbrunner, American author, coach, and speaker

Clarity is crucial. The clearer you are about what you want, the more likely you are to obtain or earn it. That's true whether you're clear about the negative or the positive. Becoming clear is a worthwhile process. From personal experience, I have noticed that the process of becoming clear can be awkward and uncomfortable at first.

As you become clearer, a creative process begins to unfold. Each level of clarity seems to create another, higher level of clarity. A good example is writing out a vision statement. Each time I've written out a vision statement, it starts out pretty fuzzy and disjointed. After it's written out, I rewrite it. Each time I re-write my vision statement, it becomes more concise and specific. Although it still seems odd, each time my clarity reaches a certain focus level, what I've envisioned starts to occur.

The process of deciding on a career was one of the hardest I'd ever encountered. I spent countless hours going through books about various careers. Once I decided on a career and wrote down what I was going to do, within two years I was fully involved in that very career. There were several points along the path of my career at which I adjusted my vision, became clear, and watched a new branch opened up. It's a process that's difficult to explain to anyone who hasn't gone through it.

21. Leverage

> "Compound interest is the eighth wonder of the world. He who understands it, earns it, He who doesn't, pays it."
>
> Albert Einstein

Leverage is a fantastic concept. It allows a small amount of effort to create an enormous result. It's so much nicer to work smarter rather than harder. Pulleys and levers are used to move boulders and other massive objects. You can use other people's money to make a lot of your own money. You can also leverage information.

Consider some small thing can you use to create a tremendous result. A great example is what it takes for you to own your own home. You save up for a down payment, go to the bank to get qualified for a loan, find your home, close on the loan and move in. You've successfully leveraged other people's money to buy your own home. The same thing happens when you take out a loan to buy the car you want.

Getting together with other people and forming a mastermind group is leveraging ideas. It's like linking the power of several computers together into one supercomputer. The group becomes a mind. The whole is greater than the sum of its parts. Many minds are leveraged to achieve an effect grander than what could have happened as only one mind.

22. Words

> "Death and life are in the power of the tongue, and those who love it will eat its fruits."
>
> Proverbs 18:21 ESV

Words are important. They represent concepts. The unconscious mind and the quantum field respond to concepts and intention. One word can change the tide of an individual's life for the good or bad. They can bless, or they can curse.

Being positive nets positive results, and negativity creates negative effects, so choose your words carefully. Thoughts and emotions lead to words. Words represent concepts. Concepts referred to by words have enormous power to affect your mind and even the rest of the world around you.

> "But no human being can tame the tongue. It is a restless evil, full of deadly poison."
>
> James 3:8 ESV

The spoken word has the power to bless and to destroy. Never underestimate the power of your words.

If your life is anything but what you want it to be, take an inventory of the words you've been thinking and saying out loud for years, especially the words you've been using over the last couple of years. Concepts affect your thoughts and emotions. Say to yourself, "Think about a white tiger with blue eyes," and your mind will create an image of one quite quickly.

In the book of Mark, when Jesus entered Jerusalem with his disciples, He cursed the fig tree. He said no fruit would ever grow on it again. Three days later, it was withered from the roots up.

In Mark 11:24, Jesus also said we could say to a mountain to be uprooted and cast into the sea. If we believe, without doubt in our hearts, then it shall be done.

Your words can move mountains when mixed with an even small amount of faith from your heart. The good news is we're starting way smaller than a mountain. What you and I are starting with is something as simple as a thought or an emotion. Think of that as learning to ride a bike with training wheels.

Is there anything to this blessing/cursing stuff? Of course, there is. Even telling someone to have a nice day or saying "God bless you" is a blessing that will manifest positively in that individual's life.

I read about a man who had lost his wife to breast cancer, one year after he had yelled at her during an argument that he hoped she died of breast cancer. It took him several years to get over the role he played in her death once he realized that her illness began with what he said. If he'd understood the power of his words soon enough, he could have reversed it in time to save his wife's life.

In Luke 8:24, Jesus told the wind and waves to be calm, and they were.

Many who've studied this phenomenon much longer than I have believe that when your thoughts become intentions and mix with strong emotions that are verbalized, what you say is likely to come into being. According to Jesus, it seems there's a lot of truth to that. He warns us to believe that it's already happened and have no doubt in our heart. It only takes a mustard seed size of coherent faith to do it, too.

Your thoughts, developed into beliefs and intentions, mixed with intense emotion and words have created the life you live today. The same process can be used to change your life into something that you love if it isn't already. As you evaluate the thoughts and words you've used, do you notice any patterns? Do you often find yourself thinking that you knew something bad was going to happen, that you can't do anything right, or that everyone hates you?

There are too many variations to mention. The important thing to remember is that harsh words can create bad things happening to you. Change the words you speak to be positive, and your words can result in good outcomes in your life.

The phrasing of the words seems to make a difference. It appears from all I've studied that the best results happen when statements are in the present tense, rather than the future tense. For example, speaking the phrase, "I will feel calm," might not necessarily result in you feeling calm anytime soon, however, saying "I can feel calm," "I would like to feel calm," or "I must feel calm," while perhaps all true statements, create no outcome of feeling calm.

It appears that neither the unconscious mind nor the quantum field has a regard for the passage of time. In those realms, everything is only, now. Therefore, creating with words works best when phrased in the present or infinitive tense, in the "I am" form. Saying, "I am calm" creates an immediate response in your unconscious mind. Try it and see for yourself.

The next time your mind is busy and won't slow down, say the phrase, "My mind is calming down more and more until it is completely calm. My mind is still."

At the same time, imagine your mind being calm. Try it and notice what happens. Be honest. Did it even calm down a little bit? It doesn't matter if you ultimately believe what I and so many others are telling you. It's true. Jesus made it clear, too.

23. Listening

Maybe you're familiar with the acronym GIGO. It's a term commonly used by computer programmers in the early days of computer programming, and it still holds true today. GIGO stands for *garbage in, garbage out*. The input programmed into your computer determines the output. It's the same with your mindset.

Information enters through your hearing. Even if it comes through your eyes or from something you've read, it's still going into the hearing part of your brain, the auditory center. From there it influences your thoughts, perceptions, and interpretations, which all affect your beliefs and intentions. These then change your emotions.

Over two thousand years ago, Jesus made it clear that how and what we hear makes a difference in our lives, so He encouraged us to use caution when listening.

> "Take care then how you hear, for to the one who has, more will be given, and from the one who has not, even what he thinks that he has will be taken away."
>
> Luke 8:18 ESV

Our ears receive every sound produced within the range of our ability to hear. We can detect a range of frequencies from 20Hz to about 20,000Hz.

That's what our ears can do under ideal circumstances. It doesn't mean our brain pays attention to all of it though. Due to a fantastic design in your mind called the reticular activating system, you can distinguish one particular sound or voice out of a sea of hundreds. Even penguins of Antarctica can do that. A parent penguin can distinguish the sound of their chick out of thousands of others, even with the cold wind howling.

Jesus said in Luke 8:18 to "Take care then how you hear...." What does the phrase, "How you hear," mean?

After decades of teaching communication skills to thousands of clients, it's my opinion that how you hear is all about whether you're listening for accurate understanding, or to only listen to what you want to hear. Your perceptions, interpretations, beliefs, and intentions flow forth from how you've heard what was said by others, including God. If you're listening carefully for accurate understanding, your interpretations will be more truth than distortion. If you have a lot of distortion, your thoughts, emotions and other results in your life will reflect that. When you hear and understand accurately, the results will be far more orderly and positive.

In teaching communication, we talk about how it's not the *what*, it's the *how*. The *what* is usually about content, while the *how* is about the tone of voice, inflection, and implied meanings.

It's not just *what* is heard, it's *how* it's heard.

"And He said to them, 'Pay attention to what you hear: with the measure you use, it will be measured to you, and still more will be added to you.'" Mark 4:24 ESV

Jesus also said to be careful what you hear. If you can tune your hearing for how you listen, you can optimize your understanding of what you hear. It's like adjusting a search filter on the internet. You can change the search for what you're looking for in an ocean of what you don't want to find. If you're looking for the negative, you'll find it. When you're looking for the positive (what you want), you'll see it. When you don't know what you're looking for, who knows what you'll find?

To create results of what you'd rather have in life, tune the search engine of your listening app in your brain to be more selective. Refine your search to what would serve you in a positive and joy-giving way. It can happen. Be careful about what you're seeking because you'll probably find it.

24. Faith

> "So faith comes from hearing, and hearing through the Word of Christ."
>
> Romans 10:17 ESV

There are several different definitions of faith floating around the world. The meaning of a word that matters the most is what the speaker meant when they used the word in the first place. Some have defined faith as just another word for "trust," or "belief." Considering faith to be just another word for trust or belief doesn't make sense. Jesus didn't use the words faith, trust, and belief interchangeably. Therefore, they are three different words.

The best working definition of faith that I've come up with in my life is that faith is agreeing with God. Trust and belief are involved in that agreement, and that's how the three words are related.

Believing what God says and trusting God are forms of faith. The faith that pleases God isn't something that we seem to be able to muster up on our own. We need God's help. Faith comes by hearing the Word of Christ. The seed comes from God, is planted into us, takes root and grows.

According to Jesus, when you have faith the size of a mustard seed with no doubt, you can move a mountain. I believe that you can literally move a mountain. Most of the changes that you want to create are smaller than a mountain, although they can sure seem that big sometimes. Changing anxiety into calmness, depression into joy, poverty into wealth, and a bad relationship into a great relationship requires less faith than what it takes to move a mountain. Start small and work your way up.

25. Silence

> "Silence is a source of great strength."
>
> Lao Tzu, ancient Chinese philosopher and writer

Most people are uncomfortable with silence. In graduate school, we were taught to respect silence. In one of my earliest sessions, my client was silent for 45 minutes. Neither of us spoke. At the end of the visit, he wrote out a check. I almost handed it back to him because we didn't "do" anything, but he told me that was the best fifty dollars he'd ever spent.

That was a lesson for about just how powerful silence is. It allows your mind and soul to relax and clear itself out of all the input it receives on a constant loop. It creates a space for you to hear your inner voice as well as God's still, small voice.

26. Surrender

> "Let God have your life. He can do more with it than you can."
>
> Dwight L. Moody, American evangelist and publisher

The Stress/Performance Curve from Chapter 6 illustrates how it's possible to try too hard. Working harder can make things worse at some point. There comes a time when you've put everything out there, but nothing's working. That's time to surrender, especially to God. Sometimes things aren't working because you and God aren't compatible, and God doesn't change. There can be a lot of peace when you surrender. Resistance calms down. It's a chance to tune in and find a better path.

I was pretty sick as a child. I learned early on to just surrender and let my body heal. It seems to be counterintuitive to most people. Surrendering doesn't mean to agree with the sickness. It means to stop resisting and avoiding. In some ways, it's like finding your way out of a Chinese finger puzzle. One side has to surrender to get both fingers out.

27. The Power of God

> "For God gave us a spirit not of fear but of power and love and self-control."
>
> 2 Timothy 1:7

Any consideration of God's power begins with Genesis 1:1, "In the beginning, God created the heavens and the earth." Everything starts there. Where no heaven or Earth existed before, there does now, by the power of God. God is the source of all real energy. If you hang around Judeo-Christian groups, you'll hear the phrase, "the power of prayer," mentioned occasionally. Prayer is when you talk to God.

I'm sure some would say I'm splitting hairs here, but the power of prayer is still God. Everything God has done from the beginning is relational. He wants a relationship with you and me. Reading The Bible makes it very clear that God is available to you and me every day. There are conditions to having God's power in your life. Meet those conditions, and you avail yourself of the most vital ingredient to a life worth living. Many people agree with the statement, "One person, walking with God, is always in the majority."

Jesus said in John 15:5, "I am the vine; you are the branches. Whoever abides in me and I in him, he it is that bears much fruit, for apart from me you can do nothing." It may look like all the previous forms of power are what we have naturally within us, and that interpretation would be correct; all of them are potent aspects that every person naturally possesses.

At the same time, the power of God is available for everyone, too. Depending on your religious upbringing, that may be tough for you to believe. A straightforward Biblical interpretation shows that God is going out of His way to be available to every one of us. God is relentlessly pursuing each one of us.

Jesus demonstrated God's power to heal, to cast out demons, to increase resources such as food and money, and ultimately save any soul for eternity who is interested. If you're a person who would prefer to do it solo, then there's no need to read any more of this chapter. You can skip to the next section.

There's a great deal you can apparently get done on your own. Multitudes throughout history have proven that to be true. You can be wealthy, happy, and have a life you love, even without God. But, Jesus also said, "What shall it profit a man if he gains the whole world and loses his own soul?"

What you achieve in this life is only temporary. When you die, you live on for eternity. Where you live is optional depending on the choices you make with God now. To surrender to God and His plan is to make you available for His wisdom, guidance, presence, and power. God is gentle and kind and will not force Himself on you.

God's power isn't like a magic wand. So many people have given up on God because He's not serving them like they think He should. They've got it upside down and backward. Expecting God to serve them implies that they're God and that God is their servant, so no wonder they're disappointed.

Remember, the power of God is available 24/7.

PART THREE
THE PROCESS

CHAPTER NINE
ROMANCING THE PAIN: MAKING PAIN YOUR SERVANT

Your Relationship to Pain

"Pain is inevitable. Suffering is optional."

Unknown

Pain is no fun. It hurts. When something hurts badly enough for long enough, it can suck out a lot of energy. Pain can be physical and emotional. Emotions can create symptoms of illness in the body. Pain in the body can bring about emotional responses.

What in the world does any of this have to do with pink elephants and white tigers? It has a great deal to do with it in every way. Pain can be a type of obstacle much in the same way that anxiety is an obstacle for most of us. It's uncomfortable, and it's obstructing the enjoyment of life. It's tempting to think that pain is the problem. It's not. There's more to it than that.

I learned in my undergraduate training that the mind doesn't recognize the difference between physical pain and emotional pain. Pain is pain.

Watch an 18-month-old child fall and skin their knee. You'd think someone tried to take their leg off without anesthesia. Their yelling can rattle the rafters. When that child is three or four years old, it's much the same. Now, notice a six-year-old out the kitchen window in the yard after they've skinned a knee. They look around, their lip quivering, to see if anyone noticed. Once they realize nobody is going to make a fuss about their war wound, they go about the business of playing. A few years later, when that child is now ten years old, they come in and get ready for bed. You notice a big gash on their leg and ask them what happened. The ten-year-old merely shrugs and says they don't know," as if it's irrelevant.

The relationship to pain has changed over the years. It's transformed from something interpreted as being life-threatening and horrible, to a mere nuisance. Contrast this with the multitude of souls who've experienced various levels of hurt, from mild to severe. Most of them have been nursing that pain for many decades.

They'll tell you stories about how they can no longer trust anyone, or how life will never be good again because of all that unresolved hurt. They create walls around their heart and grow thorns outside of the wall. Decisions are made to avoid intimacy and to preemptively push others away before any potential injury happens to them. Every strategy serves to protect them because of an implication that there's no way that they can handle the pain of hurt. They're too fragile.

However, if the mind doesn't recognize the difference between physical pain and emotional pain, then why aren't they walking around with bubble wrap around their knees just in case they fall? Pain is nothing more than pain. How can you endure one kind of pain but not the other? It's because of what you tell yourself, not because of the pain itself.

Why not just go into your mind to correct the false beliefs about being hurt, forgive the person that injured you, and move forward? Allegedly, it's because you might get hurt again. To move on would require personal responsibility for your thoughts, feelings, and actions. It would require giving up any benefits of having an unhealthy relationship with pain.

You get more of whatever you focus on. As a result of pain, you might come to develop negative beliefs about yourself, the world, and others, and those beliefs can result in damaging negative emotions.

A friend of mine recently gave an example of how the white tiger process can help with pain. She was working with a person who'd been injured in a recreational vehicle accident several months prior. The client had a great deal of pain all over her body from the accident. My friend wanted to help her reduce the pain. She asked her client to identify where in her body she felt no pain.

The woman had to think a bit. She eventually noticed that her left ear had no pain. As she identified more and more areas of her body that had no pain, her overall experience of pain continued to reduce.

The strategy is brilliant. Focus on any location in your body where there is no pain. Find and list as many areas as you can. In a short period, the pain becomes diminished, and eventually, the only pain you're aware of is a fraction of what you'd been experiencing only moments before.

The Aspects of Pain

The main aspects of pain are past remembered pain, future anticipated pain, what the pain means to you, what the pain implies about you, and finally, pain itself.

The actual pain is only twenty percent of the overall pain complex, which means that if something about the first four aspects could adjust, there would be an eighty percent reduction in the experience of pain.

Some studies from the 1980s and 1990s have shown that chronic pain clients tend to experience their pain as continuous. In their mind, the pain was happening twenty-four hours a day, seven days a week.

Those who have volunteered to have their pain monitored with more scientific equipment such as electromyography, heart rate, EEGs and so on, allowed researchers to look into how true their experience of pain actually may be. After reviewing the results, researchers concluded that chronic pain suffers were, in reality, experiencing pain anywhere from one to maybe a few hours per day, not constant, as had been reported. They concluded that those suffering from pain had focused so much on past remembered pain that their mind had created an illusion of the pain being continuously present.

Effective hypnotists took advantage of that pattern. Eliciting a trance, they focused the client onto the time periods during which there was no pain. With some training, clients were able to create new continuities. There was no longer the experience of constant pain, only of episodic pain, which is much easier to bear than to have no hope of relief.

When clients had a perceived history of constant pain, they reasoned that the future would look as bad as the past, or worse. If they expected their pain to continue and get worse, it did. Anticipation of the pain created an intention and the patients became aimed at the pain. If someone who suffers from constant pain can shift out of that false belief and imagine a more acceptable outcome, that new outcome can emerge.

That's two of the five pieces of the pain complex eliminated.

Next, consider what the pain means to them, which can be an essential part of the process. Maybe there's a metaphor that represents what's going on in their mind, such as "It's like being a T-Rex with one arm longer than the other and walking on a foot with a thorn in it."

One picture is worth a thousand words. The metaphors that people come up with to describe their pain are frequently spooky accurate and can reveal a telling story. For instance, one person described herself as a spiny sea urchin lying on the ocean floor. As she painted a picture of the sea urchin, she revealed all the detail needed to address her pain.

The meaning of the pain is an interpretation. That interpretation can result in the creation of beliefs, emotions, and responses that can increase and perpetuate the suffering. When those interpretations and beliefs are identified and corrected with the truth, this part of the pain complex can vanish quickly. When that happens, the client often wonders what that means about them. They may fear that it says they're weak, or perhaps that they're not good enough. Using the process described earlier about focusing on what you'd prefer it means to you and about you, those self-defeating beliefs can efficiently shift.

Now we've removed four out of the five aspects of pain. There's no need to see a hypnotherapist to do that unless you want to. Using the power of choosing your focus, you have everything you need to accomplish the same thing. The only aspect remaining is the pain itself, which is only twenty percent of what was there before!

In over half the cases of which I'm aware, even that twenty percent no longer remains after applying an excellent white tiger process. Unless there's a significant physiological cause for the pain, many times using a tool such as tapping, self-hypnosis, or mental rehearsal, it's possible for the rest of the pain to diminish until no pain at all remains.

Romancing the Pain

Not everyone who sees a helping professional honestly wants to improve. That has been a tricky reality for me to accept over the last thirty years. It was repeatedly evident as I worked with more and more clients. So many of them would come in with significant psychological, emotional, or physical pain and virtually beg for help. A large percentage of them had been to several helpers, only to find little or no improvement. Not only did they have their pain, but reportedly the pain was getting worse.

After applying techniques that I knew for a fact from experience should work quite well, at least twenty percent of them would get no better. It didn't seem to matter if they took potent painkillers, used tapping, EMDR, hypnosis, or any other method. When you work with a whole lot of people with similar issues over time, you begin to notice patterns. I witnessed a trend.

My clients were having a love affair with their pain. They were nurturing it, petting it, and giving it a great deal of attention. Although they said they wanted relief from it, apparently nothing could be further from the truth. The sufferer's entire identity relied on their relationship to the pain. If they were to heal and no longer have pain, they wouldn't know who they are. There would be a crisis of identity if the pain were to take a hike. The threat of the pain of not knowing who they are is worse than the pain they already have.

For a pink elephant person, the focus is on the pain. It's so much a part of their awareness that they can't imagine life without the pain. Becoming a white tiger person involves changing the focus to who they desire to be while the pain is somewhere else, and what better place to focus than where there is no pain? However, for that to become a reality, they'd have to divorce themselves from their lover, now identified as pain.

You can imagine how firmly most people will deny that they have a love affair with pain, even though it's evident to everyone who knows them. They can see it in others but loathe the idea that they could be that person.

Secondary Gain

Secondary gain means that some people get a benefit from their pain that they are reluctant to give up in order to overcome the discomfort.

The textbook example is someone who suffers an injury on a job. Let's presume a man has injured his back and is in a lot of pain. The doctor works carefully with him over a few weeks or months while he remains out of work. There may be surgery, some physical therapy, medication, and maybe some chiropractic work.

After a while, the doctor announces that the man is fit to return to work, however he claims to continue to experience pain. The doctor puts him through a few tests and refers him to a psychotherapist. The man is furious that the physician treats him as if it's all in his mind. The pain is real.

However, the therapist figures out pretty quickly that the man hates his job, so he helps the man find a better job, and the pain is gone. The man claims it's a miracle.

The truth of the matter is that the employee's unconscious mind was the culprit creating pain signals. He hated his job and didn't want to go back. Part of his brain reasoned that if his pain could continue, he could stay home and binge on Netflix indefinitely. The conscious part of his brain was completely unaware of the internal conspiracy. Although the pain signals were real, there was no medical cause. Having a benefit from having pain or any other negative symptom is a form of competing intention.

Illness Identity Disorder

There's no official diagnosis called, "illness identity disorder." It was made up by someone to refer to a common problem, namely that some people have come to base their identity on being ill. Have you ever experienced an identity crisis? Not knowing who you are is a frightening feeling. It's a lot easier to stay with a negative identity than to go through the anxiety involved in changing it. A giant, invisible bungee cord will automatically take them back to their negative identity.

It might be difficult to make the change, but it's not impossible. As long as an identity has a basis in anything false or contrary, nothing will change. Recall from Chapter 5 the importance of your identity. Imagine yourself having a new, positive self-image based on who God says you are. The transformation can begin immediately.

CHAPTER TEN
THE PURPOSE OF PURPOSE: WHOSE PURPOSE IS IT ANYWAY?

"True happiness... is not attained through self-gratification, but through fidelity to a worthy purpose."

> Helen Keller, American author,
> political activist, and lecturer

Your Purpose

"Those who know what will always work for those who know why."

> (unknown)

Talking about your purpose can seem like some lofty, vague, philosophical idea that only the gurus and navel-gazers find interesting. You might not be able to imagine how it relates to those of us who live in the real world. Essentially, a purpose is the reason that you are who you are and why you do what you do. It also refers to the final product that you hope to achieve when you're done doing what you do.

The reason that you do something and the final product that you hope to achieve could be of varying levels of importance. When that reason is less than vital, your level of purpose may be pretty low. In the same way, a highly prized outcome could create a significantly energized sense of purpose that drives you to do and be something great, something well beyond any personal limitation you ever imagined.

Another way to refer to the reason that you do what you do is to call it your *why*. It's the answer to questions such as why you do what you do, why you have the job you have, why you get out of bed every morning, and why you behave the way you do around other people.

The answers to these and other similar *why* questions gives you critically important awareness of what pushes or pulls you along. Everyone has a why, even if it's hidden under the clutter of a lot of other competing thoughts.

There's no way to know if you have fidelity to a worthy purpose if you don't even know what it is yet. Once you know what it is, take an inventory of how closely you're living with it. Sorting through the rubble and figuring out your "why" is worth the effort. It'll give you a chance to re-assess and refine your most profound life driver.

Whose Why Is It, Anyway?

> "The two most important days in your life are the day you are born, and the day you find out why."
>
> Attributed to Mark Twain,
> but not authenticated

There are reasons you live life in the way you do, but did you intentionally choose that, or those, reasons? For most people, the answer is no. So many of us have picked up our *why* from other people, society, and other miscellaneous sources. Their internal GPS is taking them on a wild goose chase.

Whose *why* is driving your journey? The answer will be inspired from any of three sources: you, others, or God.

Others probably are affecting your GPS more than you or God. To be more intentional, you need to take back control of your GPS. In order to do that, you'll need to have your own answers to why you do what you do and what God's purpose is for you. To know your *why*, ask yourself what it is that you want. To know God's *why*, ask yourself what God wants for you. There's nothing wrong with doing things for other people as long as what they want isn't the sole reason you're doing it. Otherwise, you're living someone else's life.

Knowing God's *why* for you is the most ultimately fulfilling purpose possible. God's intended purpose for you will give you a destination not limited by time or space. It will give you a projection point for follow-through that goes well beyond any *why* limited by life constraints. God is perfectly fine with you having both your *why* and His *why*. In fact, it seems that the *why* you've created for yourself was likely planted there by God in the first place.

What is your *why* for you? What is God's *why* for you?

Your Purpose is Your Mission

> "If you don't know where you're going, you'll probably wind up someplace else."
>
> Yogi Berra

The word "mission" comes from the Latin word "mittere" or "missio," which means, "to send." Soldiers in the military have missions assigned to them. Churches send members on missions.

In the military, everything centers around completing the mission. It's considered vital to the overall purpose, which is winning the war. Although the mission is vital to the overall purpose, the purpose of winning the war is also the mission. Most missions are micro purposes that support the larger one.

Many companies today are advised by coaches and consultants to have a mission statement. When clearly stated and conspicuously placed, a mission statement can keep that company on the road and in the lane. Similarly, personal development coaches urge individuals, marriages, and small businesses to have a clear mission statement, as it helps keep them on track.

The more concisely phrased the mission statement, the more effective the individual or company is over time. Ideally, a mission statement is just one sentence. It's common for some companies to have statements that are a paragraph long, but it's not recommended.

If a statement is more than one sentence, there may be more than one mission. More than one mission can cause confusion.

For example, Amazon's mission statement is "It's our goal to be Earth's most customer-centric company, where customers can find and discover anything they might want to buy online."[35]

Another example is Facebook's mission statement which states "Facebook's mission is to give people the power to build community and bring the world closer together. People use Facebook to stay connected with friends and family, to discover what's going on in the world, and to share and express what matters to them."[36]

Mission statements are most effective when they're laser focused and clearly embody your central purpose. The effectiveness of the military depends on extreme clarity in each mission. The war in general and lives, in particular, are on the line.

Your Identity, A Clue to Your Purpose

> "We know what we are, but not what we may be."
>
> William Shakespeare, English poet, playwright and actor

Most adults carry around a driver's license with a picture of themselves and some information about them that's supposed to set them apart from the other 7.6 billion people in the world. Their fingerprints and maybe their DNA are probably on file somewhere. Such pieces of information is believed to clarify each person's unique identity.

However, regardless of their similarity to others, each person is truly unique. God knows and values your uniqueness more than anyone else in the universe.

Your identity is important. It's far more than just what your driver's license says. It also encompasses who you believe you are. Beliefs run both little and big programs in you that affect every area of your life. Negative beliefs create negative results, and positive beliefs produce positive results.

If you have a false, negative identity, you'll tend to *be* someone negative. If you have a true, positive identity, you'll tend to *be* someone very positive. Just like a program, your tendency to *be* one way or another can determine your quality of life. Having a clear, accurate, positive identity is vital to living a fulfilled life.

All of us have at least three identities we walk around and sleep with every day. One identity contains the facts about you such as the information on your driver's license, your gender, age, ethnic origin, economic status, and so on. This could be called your, "Objective identity."

A second identity is the identity that you've told yourself is you. It may be true or false, real or imagined, rational or irrational and is probably best referred to as your subjective identity.

Remember the lottery winners who lost all of their money in a year? The identity they had about themselves was of a poor or middle-class person. Prematurely trying to step into the identity of a wealthy person didn't sync. The identity code they'd bought into forced them to get rid of anything that didn't seem to be them, sort of a poverty identity disorder. Poverty identity disorder is similar to illness identity disorder in that anybody suffering from it is allowing themselves to be defined by a negative.

There's a third identity that even most Christians don't realize they have; it's the identity God has for you. This is best referred to as your ultimate identity.

Whatever identity you embrace will program your thoughts, feelings, and actions in life. You'll tend to drift in any direction that supports your identity. You'll manage to get rid of anything that doesn't match up with that identity.

It's self-reinforcing, and because of that, it's essential that you upgrade your internal understanding of your actual and ultimate identity. The real truth about who you are is probably far better than what you've believed about yourself.

If your subjective identity is driving you and isn't in sync with your ultimate identity, it's pretty much impossible to have a very meaningful life. The truth about who God says you are is infinitely superior to anything we've typically imagined.

Who God knows you are is part of The Zone. The more in sync your acceptance of your identity in God, the more in The Zone you are, spiritually.

Here's a partial list of who we are in Christ, created by Graham Cooke in his DVD set called *The Mind of a Saint*. When you're in Christ, the list applies to you:

> "We're a new creation,
> We're a people of His possession,
> We're a Royal Priesthood,
> We're alive to God,
> All Grace abounds towards us,
> All sufficiency is in us through Him,
> All things belong to us,
> We are ambassadors,
> We are the anointed,
> We are the apple of God's Eye,

As He is, so are we in this world,
We're baptized in One Spirit,
We're baptized into Christ and His death,
We're being perfected,
We are the beloved,
We're completely blameless
We're totally blessed,
We're blessed with all spiritual blessings,
We have confident, bold access to the throne of God,
We're as bold as lions,
We're born again,
We're the bride,
We're buried with Christ in His death,
We have a Holy Calling,
We can do all things through Christ,
We're the chosen,
Christ indwells us,
We have the fullness of God within us,
We are Co-Heirs with Christ,
We are created for good words,
We're curse-free,
We're dead to sin,
We're dead with Christ,
We're declared holy,
We're disciples,
We are the elect,
We're totally enriched in all things,
We are faithful,
We are fellow citizens of God's household,
We're free,
We've got freedom from sin,
We're being freely given all things,
We're friends of Christ,
We're fruitful,
We're gifted,

We are the habitation of God,
We have the mind of Christ,
He has been made rich because of us,
He is at work within us,
He is for us and not against us,
We're healed,
We're hidden with Christ in God,
We're highly favored,
We are His fullness,
We are His possession,
We are His workmanship,
We are a Holy Nation,
We're a Holy Priesthood,
We're increasing in the knowledge of God,
We are inseparable from the love of God,
We're jewels,
We're joint heirs with Him,
We're justified,
The Kingdom of God is within us,
We're kings, priests, and rulers,
We're known by Him,
We lack nothing,
We are the light of the world,
We live by faith,
We live by God's Word,
We're living stones,
We're made in God's image,
We're the righteousness of God in Jesus,
…We're absolutely worth of who God is."
Talk about an identity!

What if you authentically believed that you're profoundly loved and favored by God? Would that get you closer to a life worth living, even if you haven't won the lottery? It's already who you are. It's my understanding that when someone asked Michelangelo how he created the statue *David*, he said something to the effect that he just chipped away anything that didn't look like David. To Michelangelo, David was already in the stone.

In the same way, you're already who you are and who you are to God is pretty amazing. Now it's time to upgrade that amazing person.

CHAPTER ELEVEN
TIME TO TRANSFORMATION: WHERE LIFE BEGINS

Transforming You

It's vital to keep in mind that the goal isn't to get rid of anything. The goal is to transform. By starting from the innermost part of your being, the rest of your life can be transformed. A tiny amount of inner change can create a substantial outer result.

When learning to fly an aircraft, the flight instructor would tell you that when as little as one degree off in your heading the aircraft can wind up hundreds of miles off course in just a few minutes, depending on how fast you're flying.

It happened to me once when piloting a Grumman Tiger to Kingman, Arizona. I'd gotten distracted by a checklist of items I was tracking. A few minutes later

I decided to check my progress in flight and realized that what I saw with my eyes down below in no way matched up with my aeronautical chart. I followed my training and reasoned from the point that I last knew my location and estimated how long it'd been. Within about three minutes I realized I was at least fifty miles off course.

I corrected and eventually found Kingman just fine. Regardless, it was unsettling. It's a matter of discipline for a good pilot to be clear about their destination and all of the landmarks, frequencies, and guidance technology along the way. A good pilot also scans continuously to make sure they're on course.

Unfortunately, most people don't know they're off course. Some of them don't' even have a course because they have no destination in mind. To transform yourself, begin by focusing on what you're for. Be clear about where you want to be and when you want to be there. Get a good idea of where you are now. Calculate a trajectory from that place to where you want to be. Once you're clear about your desired destination, how you get there will virtually take care of itself.

You can transform your negative emotions into positive ones within minutes by clarifying how you'd prefer to feel. Negative, self-defeating beliefs can shift over a few days by clarifying what you'd rather believe. Unhelpful responses and other obstacles can be efficiently changed using tools such as mental rehearsal, the creative narrative, and grounding and centering.

A small change in your thoughts, emotions, and life vision will get you well on course for a life worth living. Once you're on the path, stay on it.

Transforming Relationships

To find an ideal spouse, begin with the end in mind. Identify the preferred characteristics that you're desiring. Phrase them in the positive and leave out any words such as "not." For example, if you say "I don't want them to be fat and bald," guess what? You're focused on "fat and bald," and that's most likely what you'll get. Instead, phrase it something like, "I want them to be tall, thin, and have a full head of hair." Be clear about what you want.

To improve your existing marriage, clarify how you'd rather your marriage be. Write it down and be specific. Start by identifying what you can change that will improve the relationship. Rather than arguing with your spouse, how would you respond if you were proactive and positive? Of course, it's possible to have a spouse that doesn't want to improve the relationship. Let that go. It's not always about you.

To improve your relationship with anyone else, start by applying the same process as you would with your spouse. At the same time, be clear about whether being in a relationship with the other person indeed is in your best interest to continue. It may be better to discontinue a toxic relationship, especially if the other person is unable to make their own changes. Although you can't choose your relatives, you can choose your responses.

To improve your relationship with God, read The Bible. Find out what God teaches about how to have a successful relationship with Him. Make it your highest priority to do that. Hang around others who are on the same course with God. That mutual support can make a tremendous difference over time.

Transforming Business

As an employee, your relationship with your employer can be improved in the same way as mentioned earlier. Clarify how you'd like the relationship to be, how you'd prefer to respond, and how you'd want to feel. If nothing improves, set your sails for finding a more suitable employer. Consider starting your own business. If you're in business for yourself, take a full inventory of what's not working out for you. Create a clear list of how you'd rather it be. Be specific.

Sometimes it's difficult to be clear without some coaching. Find a coach. Are you in alignment with a worthy purpose? Are you passionate about what you're doing? Is it who you are?

A coach can help you brainstorm every angle and create a plan for an appropriate, profitable business that fits you like a glove. Use the principles and skills discussed in this book to make as much income as you'd like starting from the innermost you and extending outward.

It's time to upgrade your life. Where will you begin?

APPENDIX A
DISCUSSION POINTS

A Life Worth Living

1. Is your life a life worth living right now?
2. If not, what are the top three obstacles in the way?
3. Share about the most significant struggle you're facing.

Chapter 1: Pink Elephants and White Tigers

1. What are three pink elephants that you have a hard time getting rid of?
2. What have you tried to get rid of them?
3. Are you willing to replace them with white tigers? If not, why not?

Chapter 2: Case Study: Tarzan

1. Share a gap you'd like to close in your life. Is it a belief, an emotion, financial, a relationship, or something else?
2. What response set do you exhibit that's not working for you?
3. With what response set would you like it to be replaced?

Chapter 3: Be Not Afraid

1. Where is the locus of control for your thoughts, emotions, and actions?
2. What's the next logical step for you to take to become a victor?
3. What would it cost you to be a victor?

Chapter 4: A Force Multiplier

1. How are other people a problem for you?
2. What would the atmosphere be like if you could have it your way?
3. With whom could you join to create a force multiplier in your world? What would you focus on changing first?

Chapter 5: Tools of The Trade

1. Which of the seven tools interest you the most?
2. What tools have you tried that have worked?

3. Which excuse is surfacing in your mind right now that would keep you from successfully using any of the tools?

Chapter 6: Finding Your Zone

1. Which side of the Stress/Performance Curve are you on in your life now?
2. Which area of the Wheel of Life would need to be improved first to get you into the zone as soon as possible?
3. What would it look like for you to be in The Zone?

Chapter 7: Bulldoze the Barricades

1. Which obstacle is in your way the most right now?
2. What have you noticed is a powerful motivator for you?
3. What is the next smallest step you can take to overcome your obstacle?

Chapter 8: The Truth About Power

1. Is being powerful a problem for you?
2. Where would it be most helpful to follow through in your life?
3. Which type of power would be the most beneficial to get you where you're going?

Chapter 9: Romancing The Pain

1. Which type of pain do you encounter the most in your life?
2. Which of the five aspects would you like to change first?
3. Do you notice any benefits from keeping any of the pain in your life? If so, what are they?

Chapter 10: The Purpose of Purpose

1. Do you know what your purpose is? If so, what is it?
2. Who are you?
3. What are the next, most straightforward steps you can take to clarify your purpose and identity?

Chapter 11: Time to Transform

1. Which category of relationship needs the most attention in your life to move you forward?
2. What change needs to happen to improve that relationship?
3. Is there a price to pay or a benefit you'd lose if you developed that relationship?

APPENDIX B
SPECIFIC EXAMPLES

Here are some specific examples of how to transform some particular areas of your life. Remember, there is no attempt to "get rid" of anything. Whatever is problematic is being changed from what you don't want to what you do want. If you focus on trying to get rid of something, you're attaching a bungee cord to it, and it keeps coming back.

Transforming a negative emotion:
    Let's walk step by step through an example of overcoming anxiety using what's taught in this book.

Step One
    Step one is to find the best adjective that describes the emotion you'd like to change. In this example, we already know we're working on transforming anxiety. The more specific the identifier, the more effective the process. If anxiety isn't the best word, then look up some synonyms until you find the best word. A word

like "uncomfortable" might work, but it's usually too vague in most cases.

Step Two
Rate the level of intensity on a zero to ten scale with ten representing the worst.

Step Three
Choose an intervention. For this example, let's say you've chosen the body proclamation tool. Before applying it, identify how you'd prefer to feel.

Step Four
Apply the intervention. Take your time and speak with sincerity.

Step Five
Re-evaluate and rate your anxiety on a zero to ten scale. Also, rate how calm you feel on a zero to ten scale. If it's where you want it, celebrate. If it's not yet where you want it, repeat each of the steps.

Realize that if your anxiety isn't a zero after a couple of tries, you may have resistance in the form of secondary gain. Take some time to evaluate what benefit you might give up if you transform anxiety into calmness. If you're willing to give it up, then repeat the process.

Transforming a negative belief:
Let's say you have a negative belief that you'd like to shift such as "I'm responsible for how others feel."

Step One
Write down the negative belief. Identify the belief that you'd rather have such as, "I'm only responsible

for how I feel and others are responsible for how they feel." Write that down, too.

Step Two
Rate how valid the new statement seems on a zero to ten scale. Ten means it's the most valid possible.

Step Three
Choose an intervention. For example, you might choose tapping.

Step Four
Apply the intervention. Your set-up statement might be something like, "Even though I believe that I'm responsible for how others feel, I deeply and completely love and accept myself."

Step Five
Re-evaluate and rate the validity of the new statement on a zero to ten scale. If it's where you want it, celebrate. If it's not yet where you want it, repeat the steps.

Beliefs may take longer to transform than emotions, but they will convert. Repeating the new, "white tiger" statement 20 to 100 times per day for several days will support you in helping the unconscious mind to re-program. If it doesn't shift entirely, ask yourself if you have resistance to accepting the new belief. What benefit would you give up if you ultimately take the new belief? If you're willing to give it up, then rinse and repeat. Keep going until your belief is reprogrammed.

Transforming a negative response set:

Step One
   Clearly identify the undesirable response that you'd like to transform. Clearly define the exact way you'd rather respond if the situation occurs again.

Step Two
   Rate on a zero to ten scale how valid the new response feels to you. Ten means you accept it as very much the way you are. Zero means it's completely foreign.

Step Three
   Choose an intervention. Two of the best tools with which to start to transform a response set is mental rehearsal and the creative narrative.

Step Four
   Apply the tools. Repeat the process 10-20 times per day for two weeks.

Step Five
   Re-evaluate; Rate the validity of the new response set on a zero to ten scale. If it's where you want it, celebrate. If it's not yet where you want it, do some troubleshooting.

Troubleshooting mental rehearsal:
   Make sure that when you begin rehearsing a new response set you don't change anything in your rehearsal. If you start changing things, it's as if you're starting over with a new rehearsal. Make sure that you only work on one response set change at a time, until you become a pro. Working on too many changes at a time creates competing focus and virtually self-sabotages the process.

Double check to identify any competing beliefs or emotions that may be interfering. Correct them before repeating. Consider adding audio. Read your narrative out loud and record it. Play the recording over and over as you drive around and do your daily duties.

Transforming relationships:

Step One
Identify what's not working in your relationship. Clearly identify how you'd rather it be. Would you like to think differently, feel differently, act differently, or be different?

Step Two
Rate the validity of the new way your relationship is headed on a zero to ten scale. Ten means it feels like it's already there.

Step Three
Choose an intervention.

Step Four
Apply any and all interventions.

Step Five
Re-evaluate and rate the validity of the new pattern on a zero to ten scale. If it's where you want it, celebrate. If it's not yet where you want it, do some troubleshooting. After troubleshooting, repeat the steps.

APPENDIX C
HOW TO DO BODY PROCLAMATION, STEP-BY-STEP

Step One: Assessment
Identify the negative emotion that you'd like to change. Be as specific as you can be. Rate the intensity on a zero to ten scale. Identify the emotion that you'd rather feel instead.

Step Two: Application
Tell each part of your body how you'd rather feel. Say it with sincerity when you voice it out loud. When addressing a joint in the body, preface your new emotion with the word, "very." For example:

"My toes feel calm, my feet feel calm, my ankles feel very calm, my calves feel calm, my knees feel very calm, my thighs feel calm, my hips feel very calm, my lower back feels very calm, my middle back feels very calm, my upper back feels very calm, my fingers feel calm, my hands feel calm, my wrists feel very calm, my forearms feel calm, my elbows feel very calm, my biceps feel calm, my small intestine feels calm, my large intestine feels calm, my liver feels calm, my stomach feels calm, my heart feels very calm, my lungs feel calm, my shoulders feel very calm, my throat feels calm, my neck feels very calm, my jaws feel very calm, my tongue feels calm, my teeth feel calm, my lips feel calm, my nose feels calm, my ears feel calm, my eyes feel calm, my brain feels calm, my hair feels calm."

Step Three: Reassessment

Rate the level of the old emotion on the zero to ten scale where zero is not at all and ten is the worst. Rate the new, replacement emotion on a different zero to ten scale where zero is not at all and ten is the best.

Step Four: Resolve resistance

If your negative emotion fails to go to zero, you may have some reluctance to letting it go. After resolving your reluctance, repeat from step one.

Step Five: Celebrate!

ENDNOTES
A LIFE WORTH LIVING

1. Dr. Norman Vincent Peal, *The Power of Positive Thinking,* (Touchstone; Reprint edition March 12, 2003)
2. Napoleon Hill, *Think and Grow Rich: The Original, an Official Publication of The Napoleon Hill Foundation,* (Sound Wisdom; Original First Edition 1937 edition December 13, 2016).
3. Robert Schuller, *You Can Become the Person You Want To Be,* (Jove, August 15, 1986).
4. Counselors are not really taught much about counseling in graduate school except accurate listening skills. Most learn how to do cognitive behavioral therapy on a primitive level.
5. *City Slickers,* Directed by Ron Underwood, (1991; Culver City, CA: MGM, Multiple Formats, Anamorphic, Closed-captioned, Color, NTSC, Subtitled, Widescreen.

PART ONE: THE PRINCIPLE

Chapter One—Pink Elephants and White Tigers

6. All names have been changed. Stories about clients are a compilation of many clients over the course of more than 30 years of experience. Any similarity to a specific person is purely coincidental.
7. Study Charles, M., Crank, J., & Falcone, D. (1990). A Search for Evidence of the Fascination Phenomenon in Roadside Accidents. Washington D.C.: AAA Foundation for Traffic Safety.
8. Study (Clark, B., Nicholson, M., & Graybiel, A. (1953). Fascination: A Cause of Pilot Error. Aviation Medicine, October, 429-440.)

Chapter Two—Case Study: Tarzan

9. "Golden Handcuffs". Merriam Webster Vocabulary. Retrieved 5 June 2018.
10. "The Power of Belief-Mindset and Success," by Mr. Eduardo Briceno. https://www.youtube.com/watch?v=pN34FNbOKXc.
11. Two passages from the New Testament illustrate this concept. The first is Romans 10:10 "For with the heart one believes and is justified, and with the mouth one confesses and is saved." The other is Ephesians 6:6, "not by the way of eye-service, as people-pleasers, but as bondservants of Christ, doing the will of God from the heart…"
12. The previous section about beliefs is an excerpt from my earlier eBook called, "The Astonishing Power of Belief: How Your Beliefs Can Transform

Your Health, Wealth, and Relationships." It's a free e-book available at www.johnmasoncoach.com.
13. Bob Proctor is a highly sought-after speaker and trainer in the power of the mind and intention. You can learn more about his teaching on paradigms from his Audible Audiobook called, "Culture Shifts and Paradigms," available at Amazon.
14. "Silly Dog Does Not Realize There is No Glass in the Door | AFV." *YouTube*. Video File. October 10, 2014. https://www.youtube.com/watch?v=Ls0WFCQXdlw.
15. By "others" I refer the reader to authors such as Lynn MacTaggart, Greg Braden, and Kieron Dowling. Lynn MacTaggart is a journalist who has taken great care to identify specific scientists and authors who's works are verifiable.
16. Walt Kelly (August 25, 1913 - October 18, 1973 was an animator and cartoonist. He was best known for the popular comic strip called, "Pogo." According to Larry Bush, Walt Kelly didn't originate the phrase, "We have met the enemy and he is us" in his cartoon strip. He said, "It was first used on a poster to promote Earth Day in 1970. Later, the artist put Porkypine and Pogo into a strip and attributed the phrase to Pogo...." Accessed June 8, 2018. (https://humorinamerica.wordpress.com/2014/05/19/the-morphology-of-a-humorous-phrase/).
17. Stephen R. Covey, *The 7 Habits of Highly Effective People*, (Simon & Schuster; Anniversary edition, November 19, 2013). Habit 5.
18. First developed by Dr. Gary Craig in the 1990s. Get his training for free at https://www.emofree.com/.
19. Psych-K®, was developed by Robert M. Williams, M.A. It's an impressive Energy Psychology

technique primarily used for the correction of false beliefs. Learn more at https://www.psych-k.com/.

Chapter Four—A Force Multiplier

20. Study (Ricardo Miguel Godinho, Penny Spikins & Paul O'Higgins). Supraorbital morphology and social dynamics in human evolution. (Nature Ecology & Evolution volume 2, pages 956–961 (2018).
21. Study (MARTHA K. MCCLINTOCK). Menstrual Synchrony and Suppression. (Nature volume 229, (22 January 1971).
22. This phenomenon was first observed by Chrisiaan Huygens, the inventor of the Pendulum Clock, what we now call the Grandfather Clock, in 1665. Later studies reported in Scientific Reports have proven what he observed to be correct. Study: The sympathy of two pendulum clocks: beyond Huygens observations, Scientific Reports, DOI: 10.1038/srep23580 .
23. Lynn MacTaggart, *The Intention Experiment*, (Atria Books; Reprint edition, February 5, 2008).
24. "General System Theory: Foundations, Development, Applications," by Ludwig von Bertalanffy, Penguin University Books, March 17, 1969.
25. Annette Capps. *Quantum Faith*, (Horizon House Publishers, August 29, 2017).
26. "The Divine Matrix," by Gregg Braden. Hay House, 1st Edition, January 2, 2008.

PART TWO: THE POWER

Chapter Five—Tools of The Trade

27. Lynn MacTaggart, *The Intention Experiment*, (Atria Books; Reprint edition, February 5, 2008), page 134-135.
28. The Intention Question is a term that I made up to refer to a specific type of question that elicits a proactive response from the unconscious mind.
29. Body Proclamation is also a term I made up. It's also a step-by-step protocol using the white tiger principle to shift from a negative to a positive emotion in fewer than three minutes.

Chapter Six—Finding Your Zone: Where the Life Worth Living Happens

30. Here's an excerpt from the website www.quoteinvestigator.com about the origin of the the quote, "If Your Only Tool Is A Hammer Then Every Problem Looks Like A Nail." Excerpt-"In February 1962 a conference of the American Educational Research Association was held and Abraham Kaplan, a Professor of Philosophy at UCLA, gave a banquet speech. Several months later in June 1962 a report on the gathering was published in the "Journal of Medical Education". The following excerpt about the speech included the earliest strong match for the adage known to QI.

    The highlight of the 3-day meeting, however, was to be found in Kaplan's comment on the choice of methods for research. He urged that scientists exercise good judgment in the selection of appropriate

methods for their research. Because certain methods happen to be handy, or a given individual has been trained to use a specific method, is no assurance that the method is appropriate for all problems. He cited Kaplan's Law of the Instrument: "Give a boy a hammer and everything he meets has to be pounded."
31. The concept of the Wheel of Life was initially developed by Paul J. Meyer, founder of Success Motivation® Institute, Inc.

Chapter Seven—Bulldoze the Barricades: Making Easy Work of Obstacles

32. According to the Merriam-Webster Dictionary, (https://www.merriam-webster.com/dictionary/Occam's%20razor), The "Definition of Occam's razor-: a scientific and philosophical rule that entities should not be multiplied unnecessarily which is interpreted as requiring that the simplest of competing theories be preferred to the more complex or that explanations of unknown phenomena be sought first in terms of known quantities."
33. Part of a quote by Teddy Roosevelt. The full quote is,"Far better is it to dare mighty things, to win glorious triumphs, even though checkered by failure... than to rank with those poor spirits who neither enjoy nor suffer much, because they live in a gray twilight that knows not victory nor defeat." It was said in his speech, "The Strenuous Life" to the Hamilton Club, Chicago, April 10, 1899.

PART THREE: THE PROCESS

Chapter Eight—The Truth About Power: A Little Bit Goes a Long Way

34. Bruce H. Lipton, Ph.D., *The Biology of Belief 10th Anniversary Edition: Unleashing the Power of Consciousness, Matter & Miracles Anniversary Edition*, (Hay House, Inc.; Anniversary edition, October 11, 2016).

Chapter Ten—The Purpose of Purpose: Whose Purpose Is It Anyway?

35. Amazon Corporation, "Earth's most customer-centric company-Amazon.jobs," Accessed June 11, 2018. https://www.amazon.jobs/working/working-amazon.
36. Facebook Corporation, "Mission Statement-Investor Relations," Accessed June 11, 2018. https://investor.fb.com/resources/default.aspx.

ABOUT THE AUTHOR

J.R. Mason has always had a passion for helping others create an empowered state to have a life worth living, regardless of circumstances. Through his writing, speaking, and coaching, he helps individuals, families, and businesses clarify how to do just that, and achieve it, in as simple a way as possible.

J.R. has been on his own journey since childhood not only clarifying who he is in God but learning to master his state regardless of stressful circumstances. In doing so, he was able to create a life worth living in situations that have devastated others with similar backgrounds. He's the manager of Renewed Life Focus, LLC, a coaching, and personal development company.

He and his wife, Elaine, are blessed with two precious adult children and a growing tribe of grandchildren.

To find out more, visit J.R. Mason at his website at www.johnmasoncoach.com, or look him up on facebook at John Mason Coaching.

www.ingramcontent.com/pod-product-compliance
Lightning Source LLC
LaVergne TN
LVHW012100070526
838200LV00074BA/3827